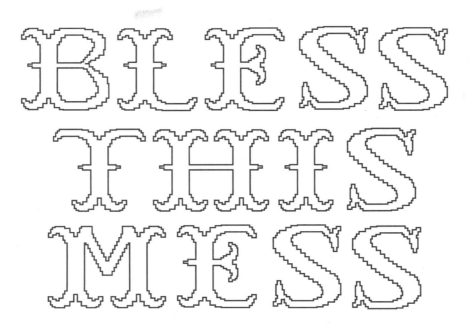

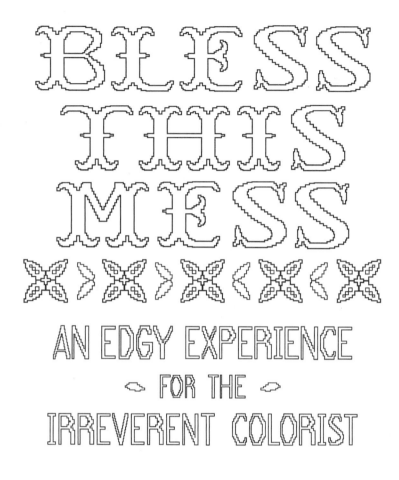

BLESS THIS MESS

AN EDGY EXPERIENCE

~ FOR THE ~

IRREVERENT COLORIST

JESSICA MAZURKIEWICZ

Racehorse Publishing

Racehorse Publishing books may be purchased in bulk at special discounts for sales promotion, corporate gifts, fund-raising, or educational purposes. Special editions can also be created to specifications. For details, contact the Special Sales Department, Skyhorse Publishing, 307 West 36th Street, 11th Floor, New York, NY 10018 or info@skyhorsepublishing.com.

Racehorse Publishing™ is a pending trademark of Skyhorse Publishing, Inc.®, a Delaware corporation.

Visit our website at www.skyhorsepublishing.com.

10 9 8 7 6 5 4 3 2 1

Cover design, cover illustration, and interior artwork by Jessica Mazurkiewicz

Print ISBN: 978-1-944686-97-0

Printed in the United States of America

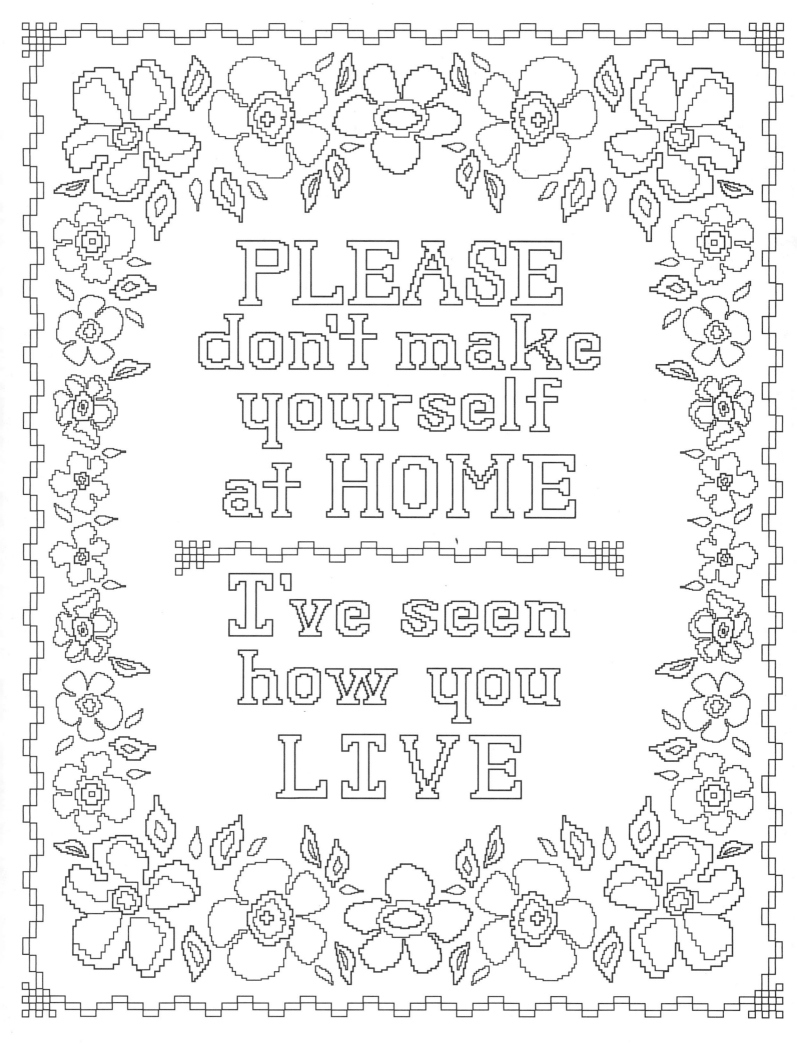

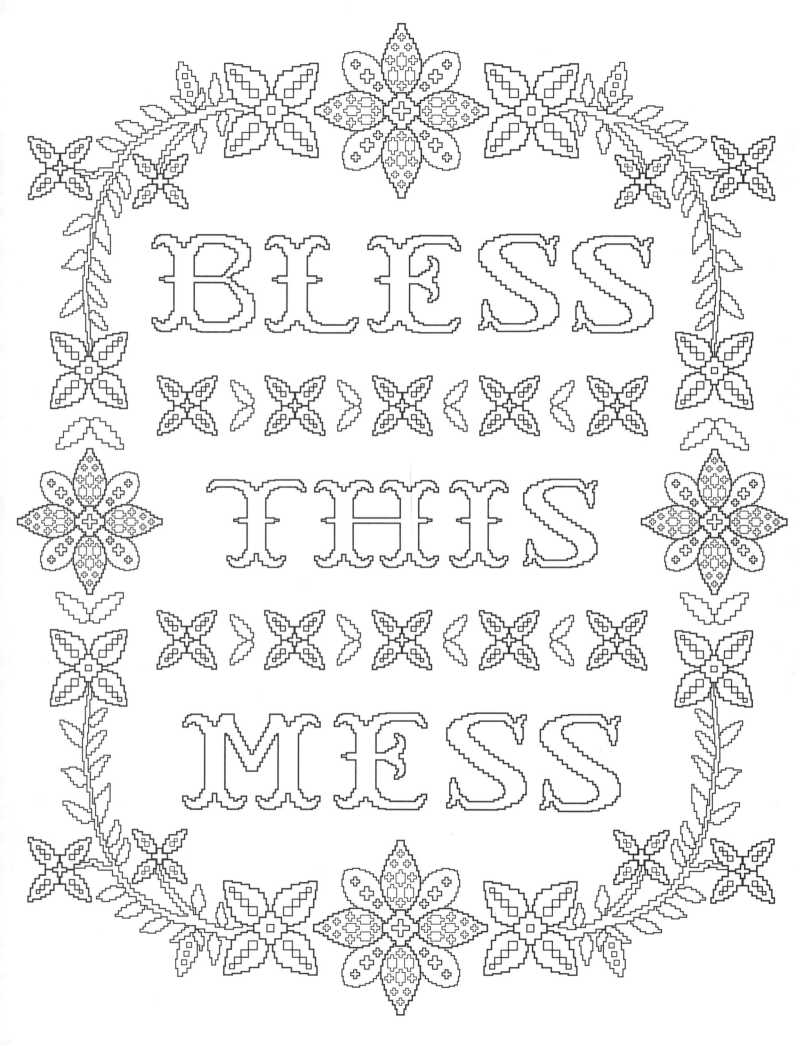

← 2

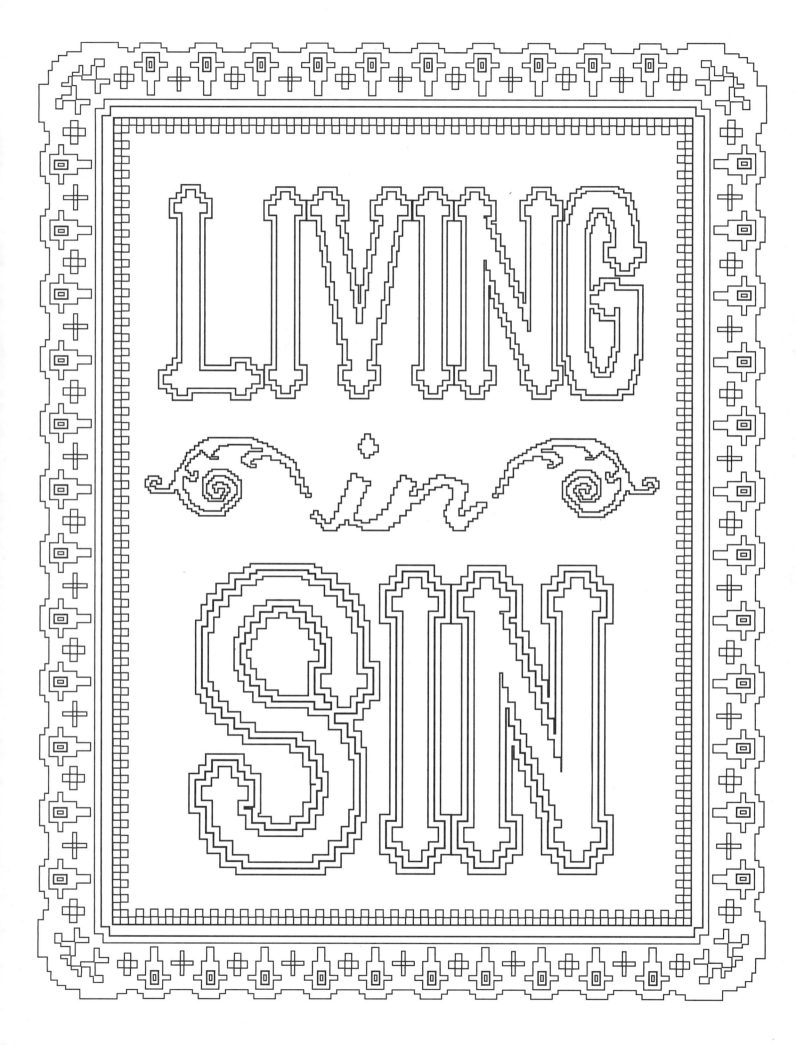

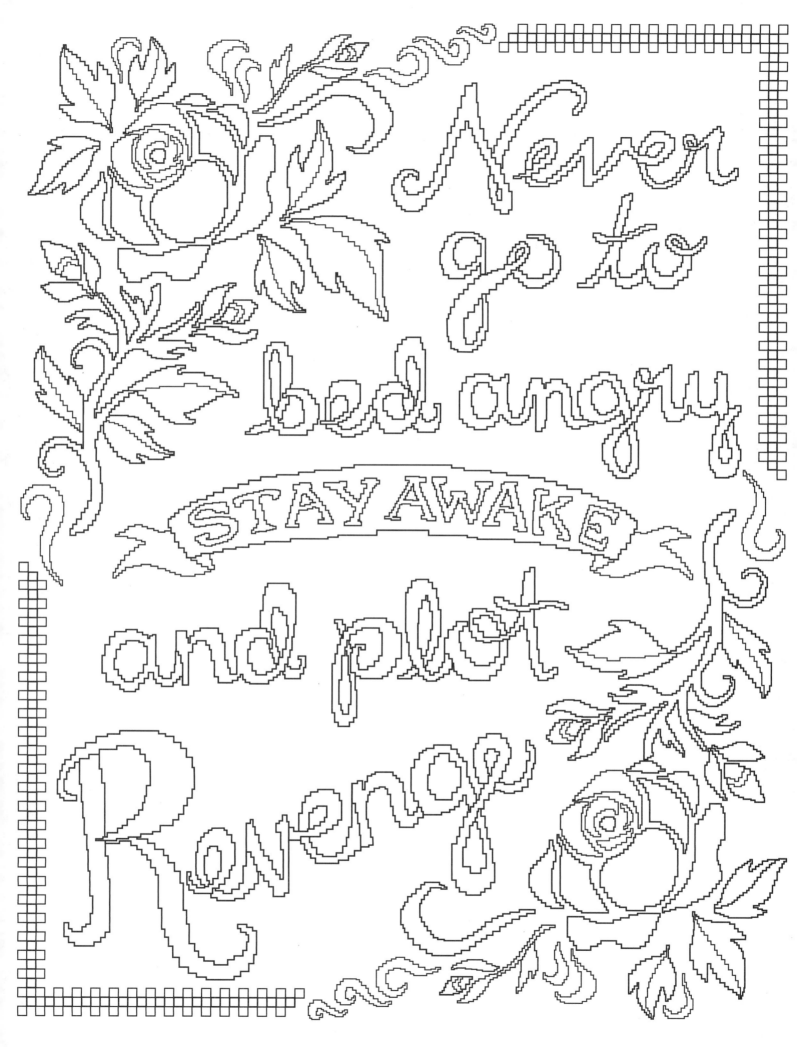

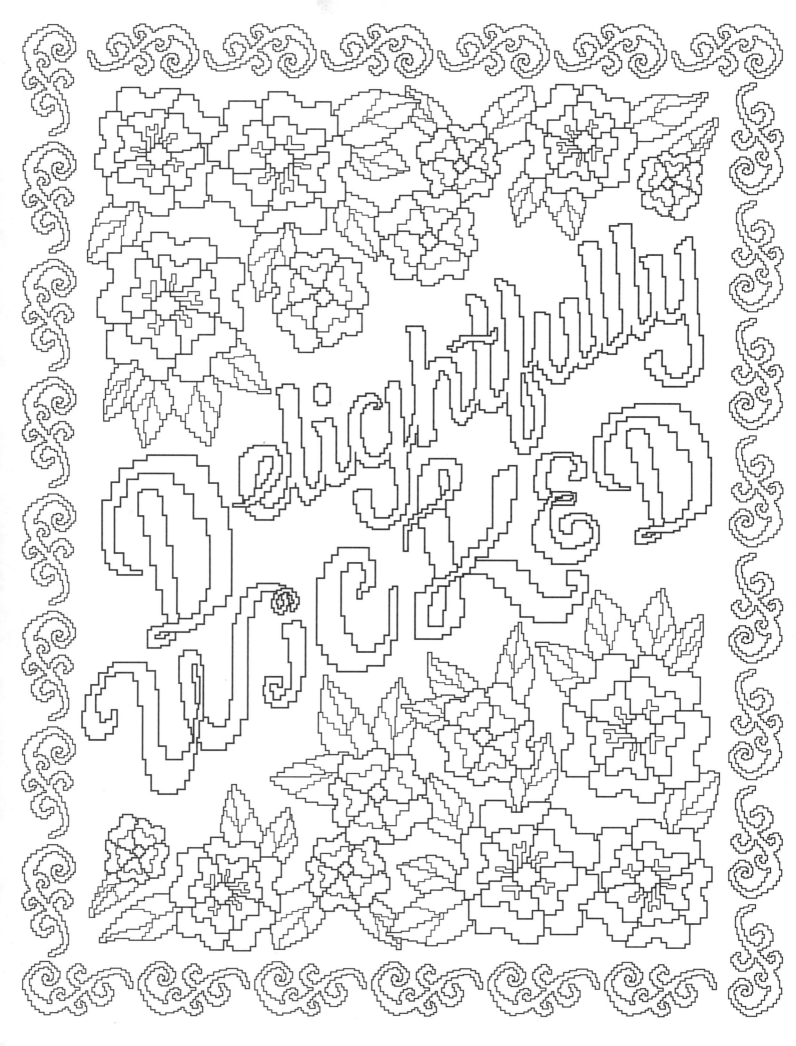

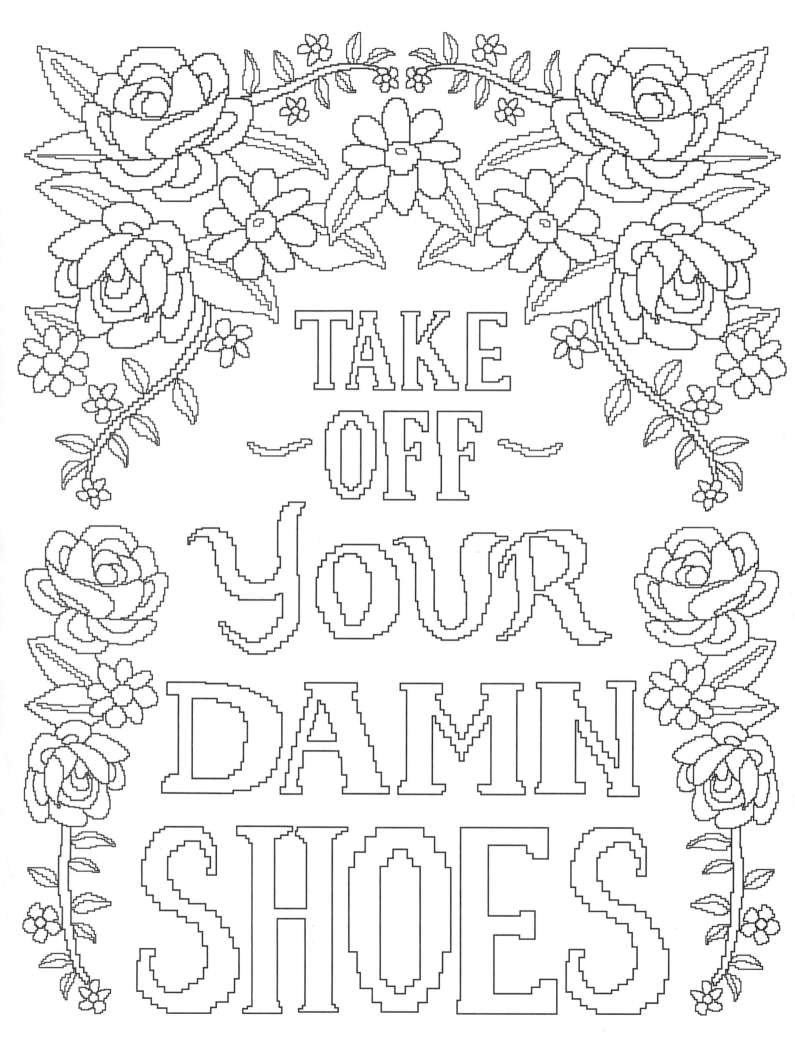

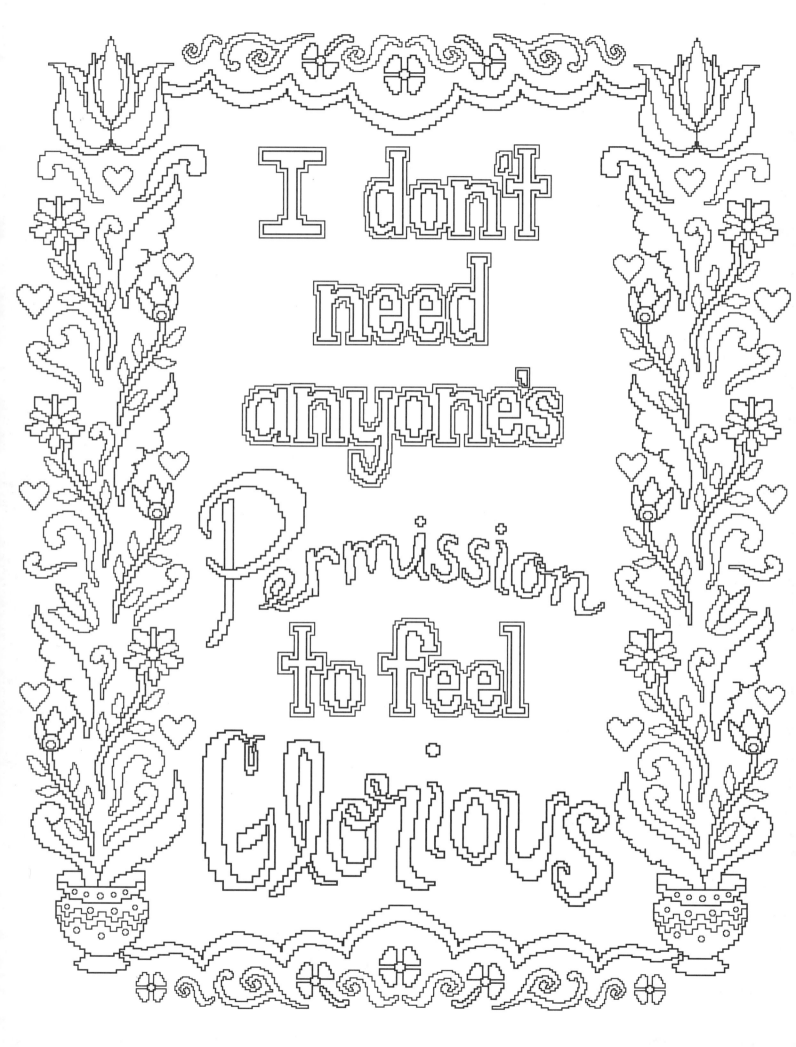

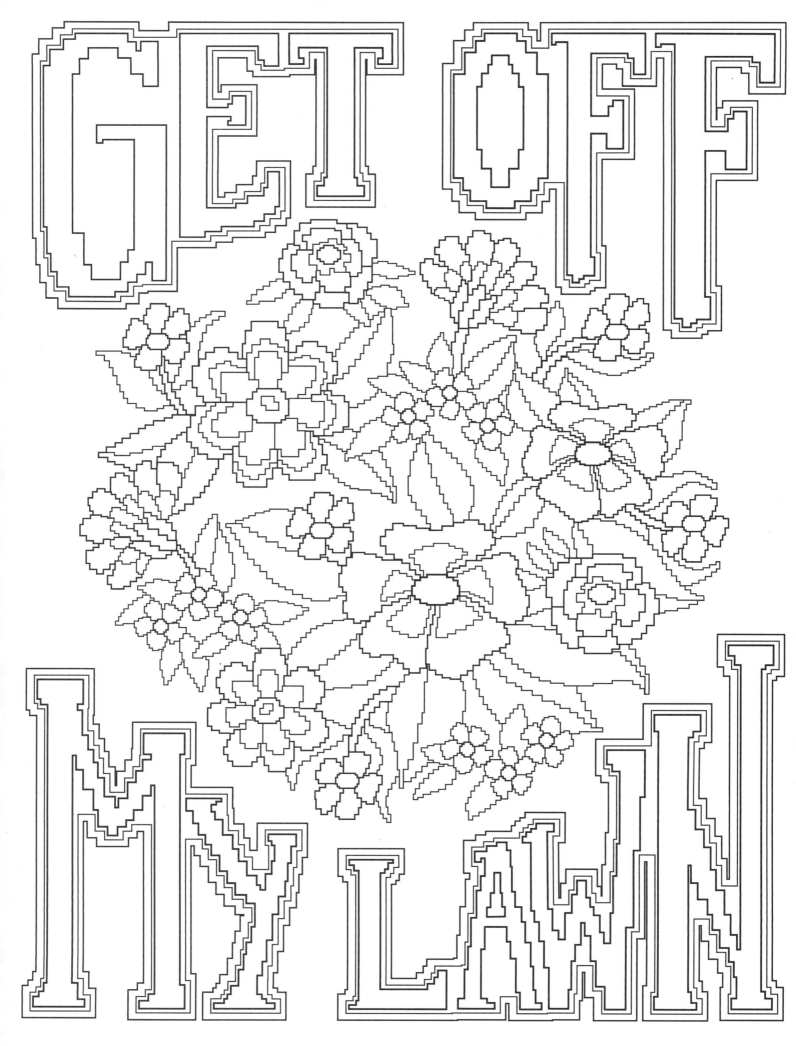

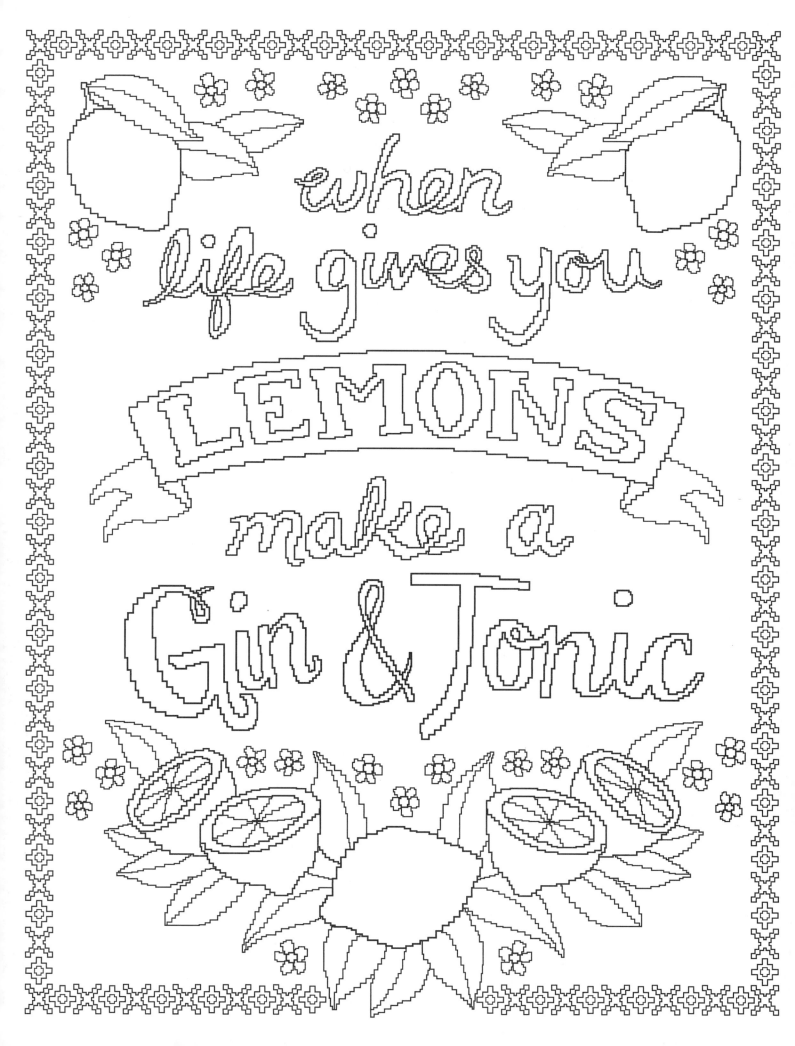

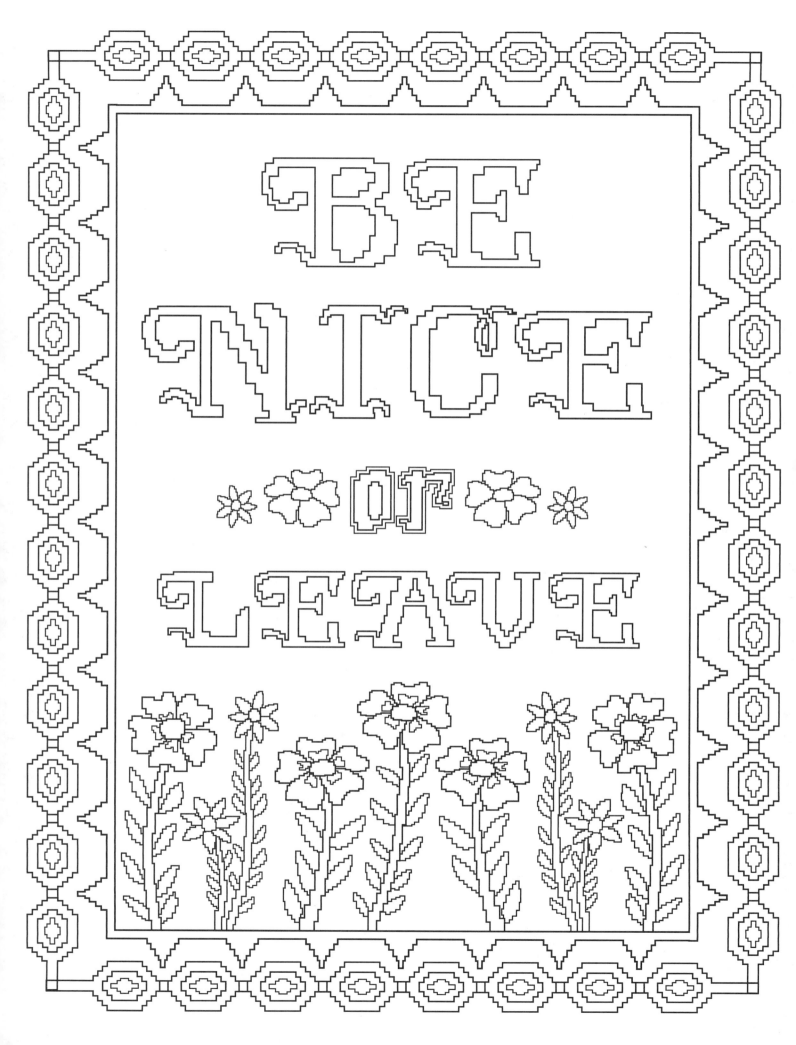

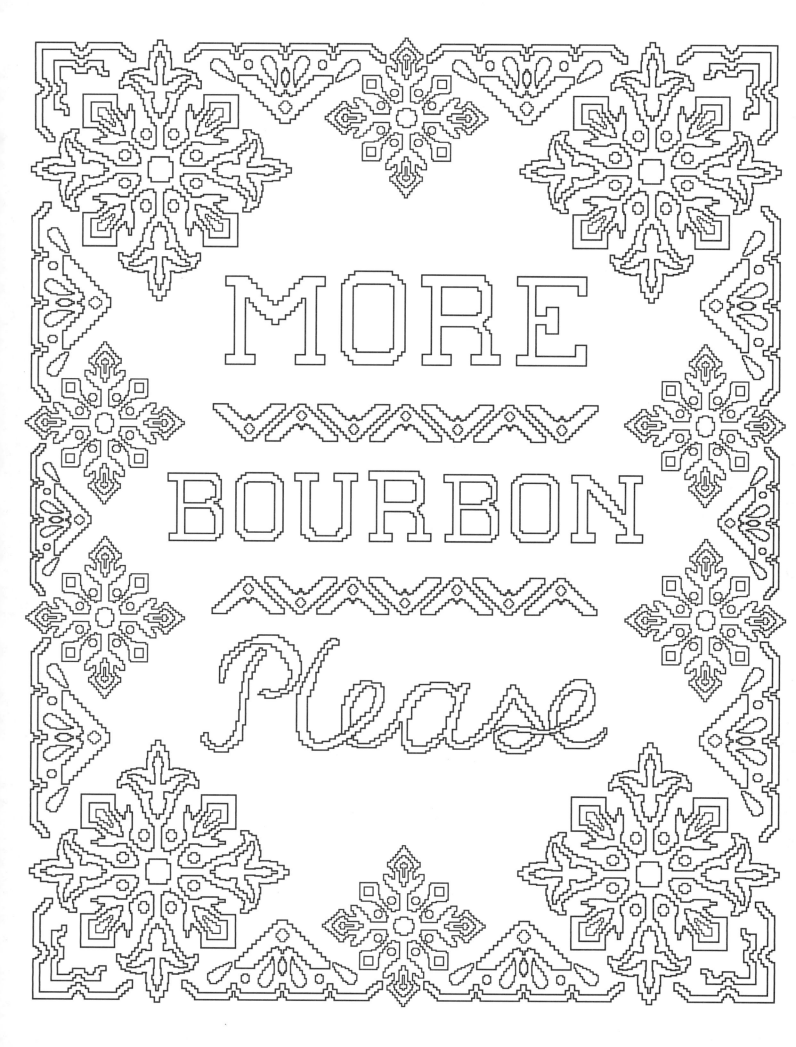

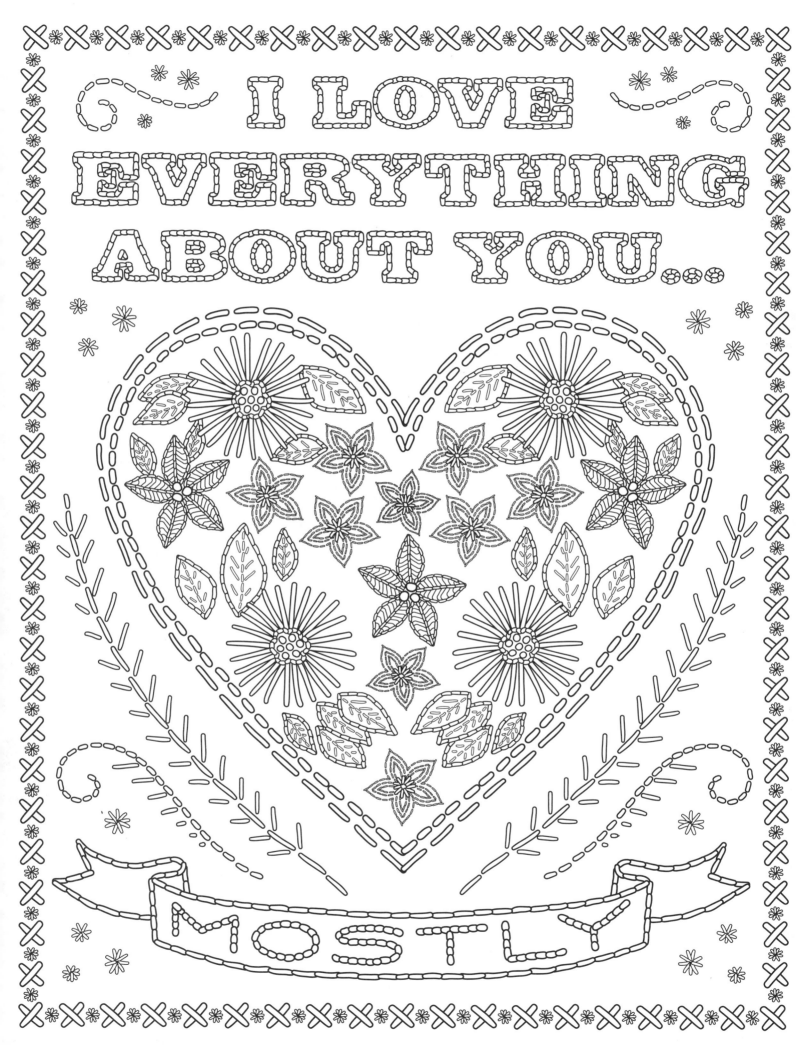

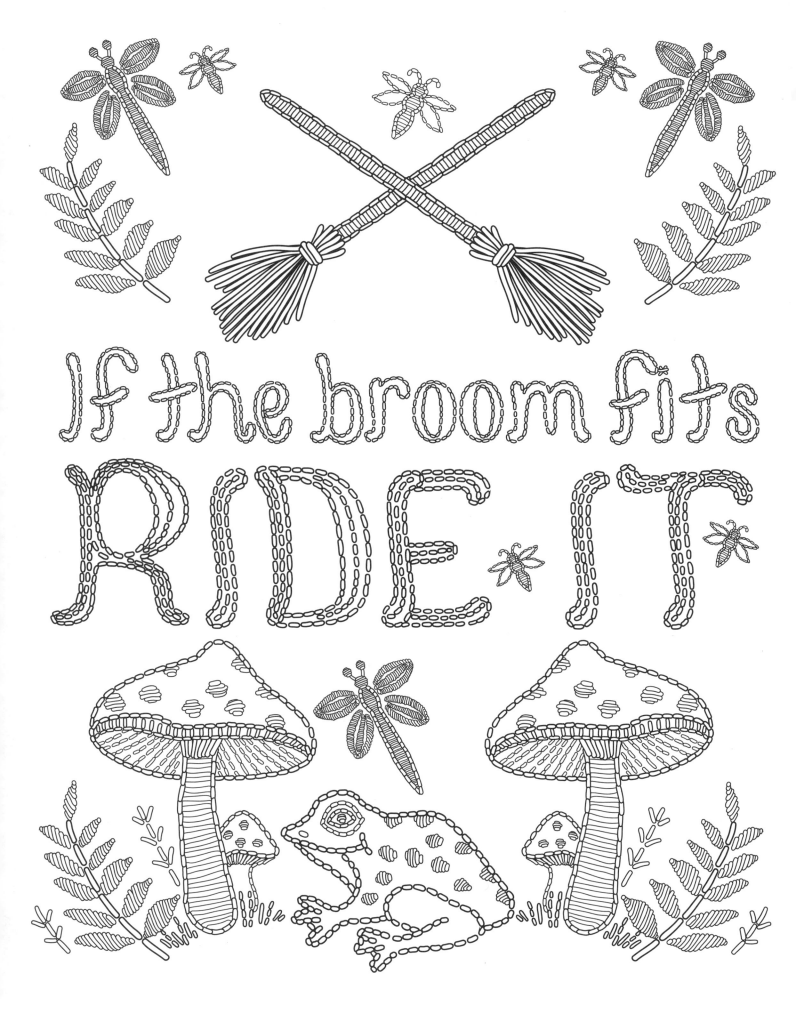

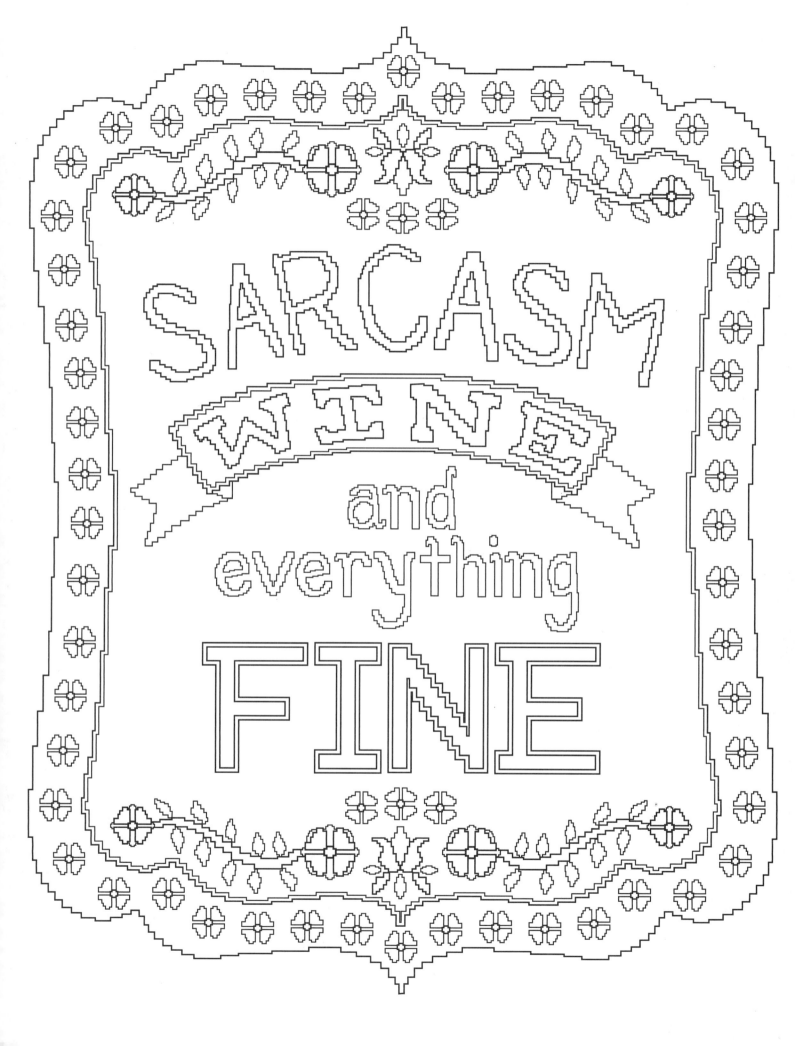

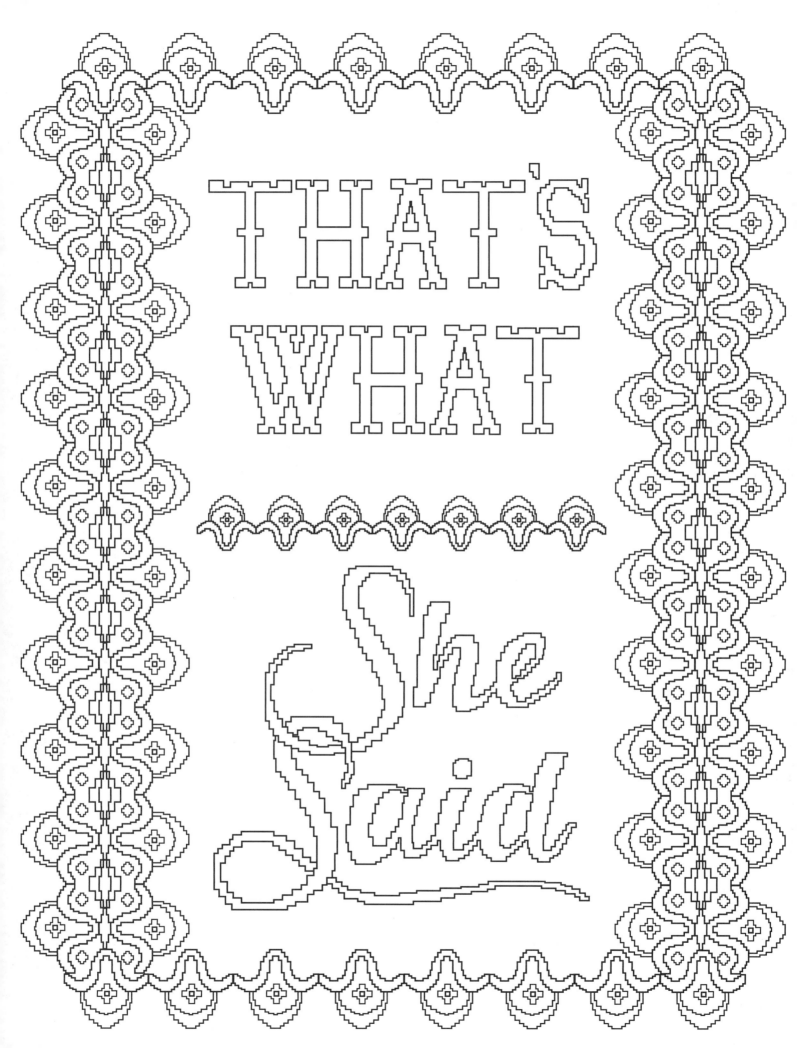

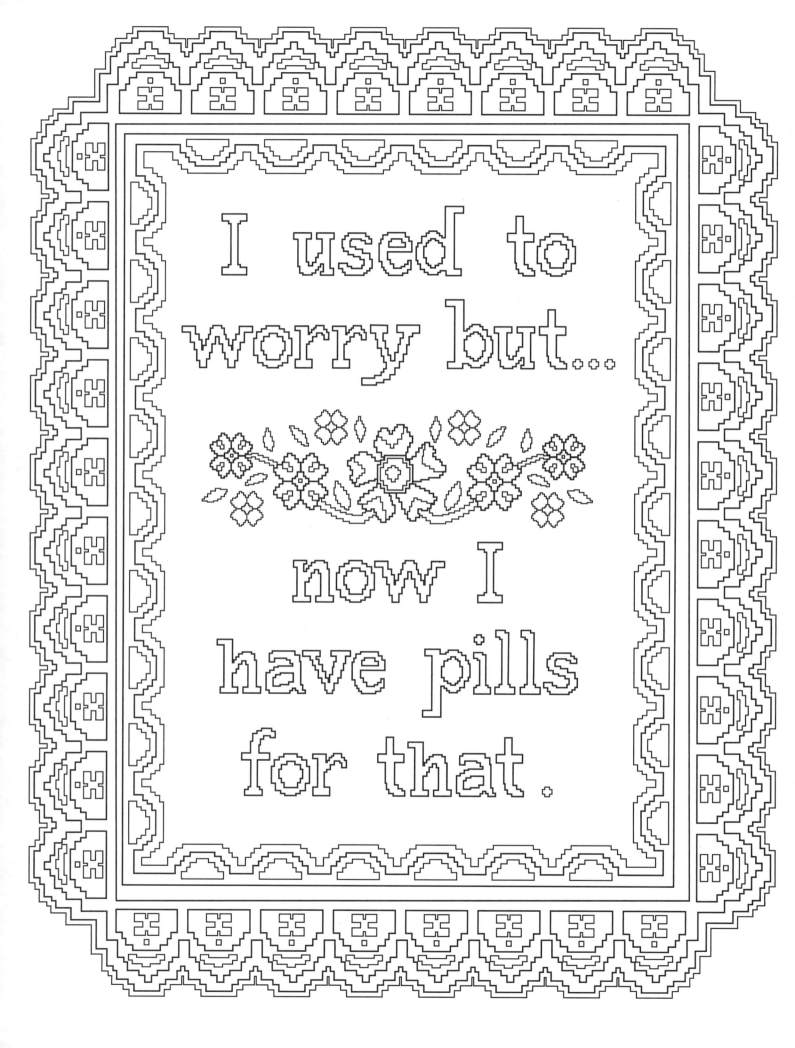

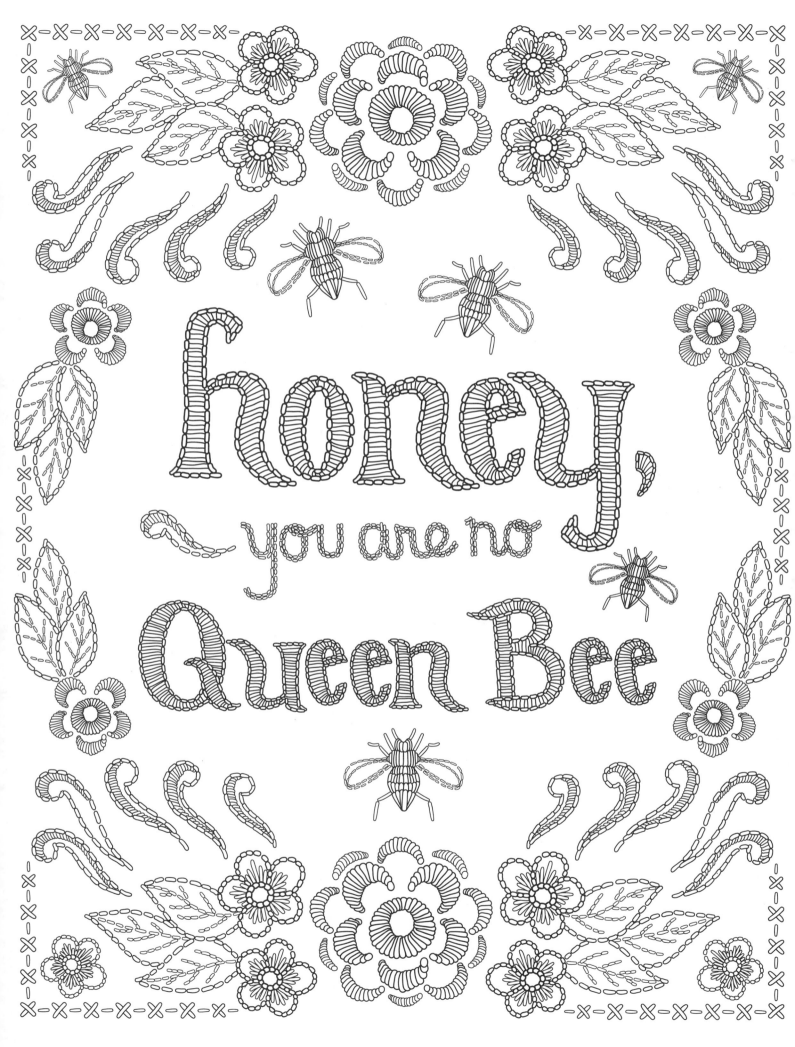

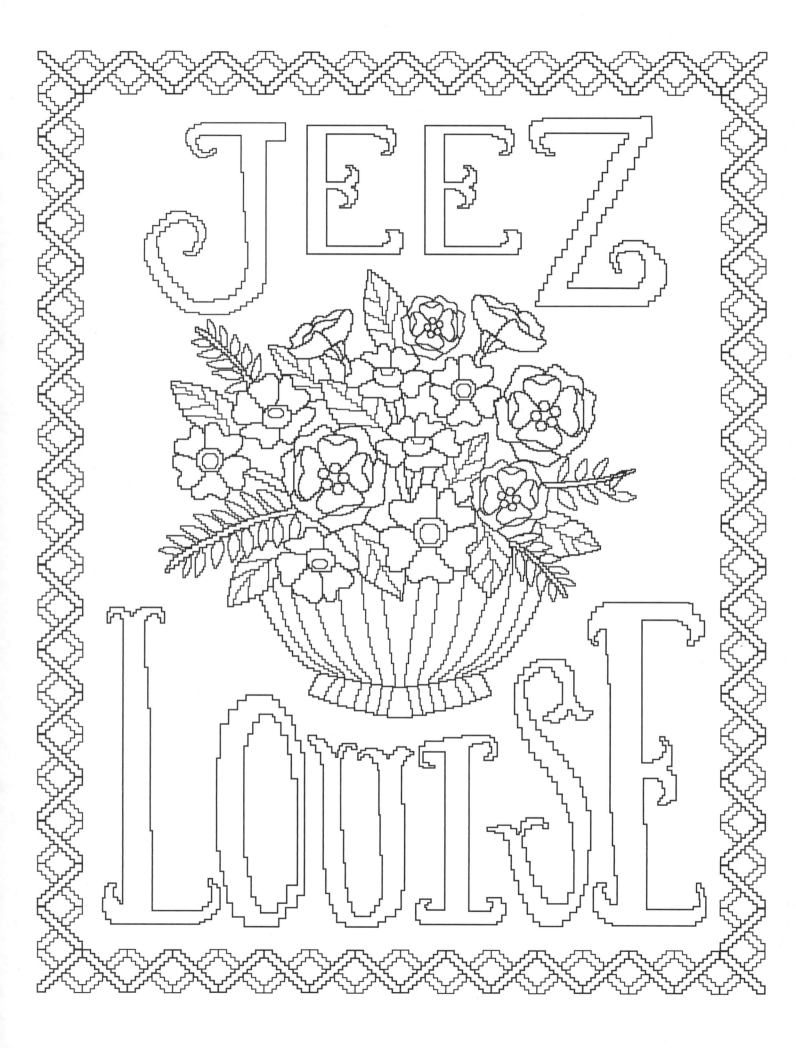

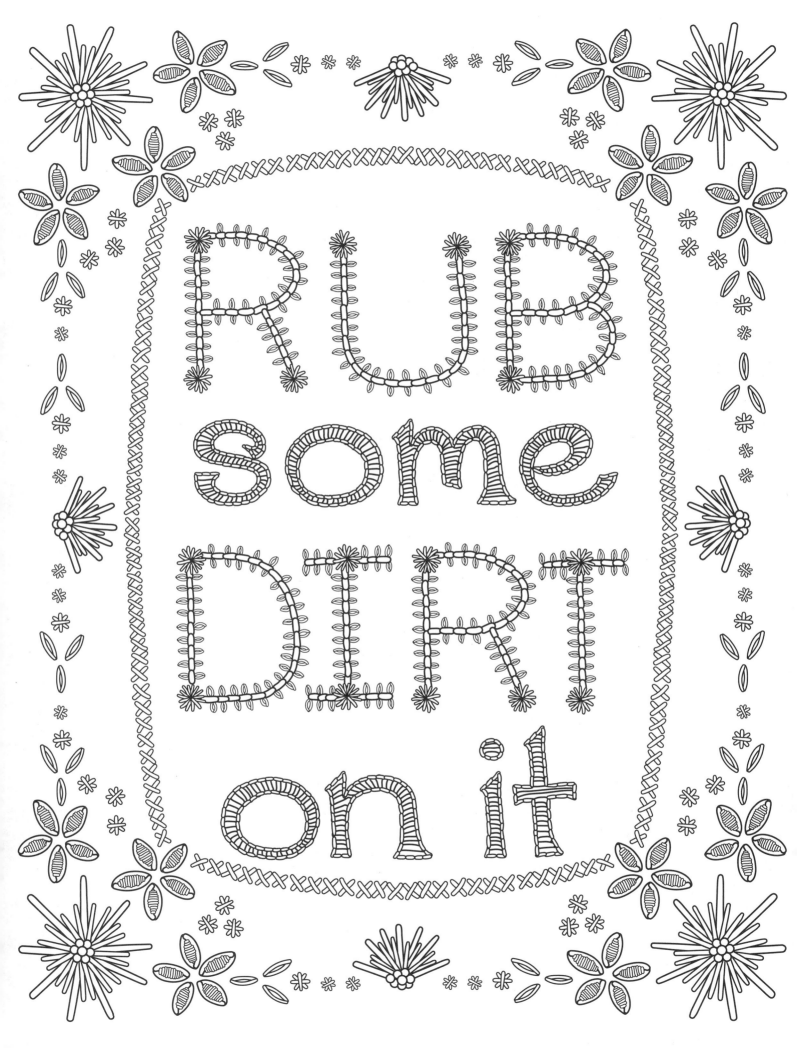

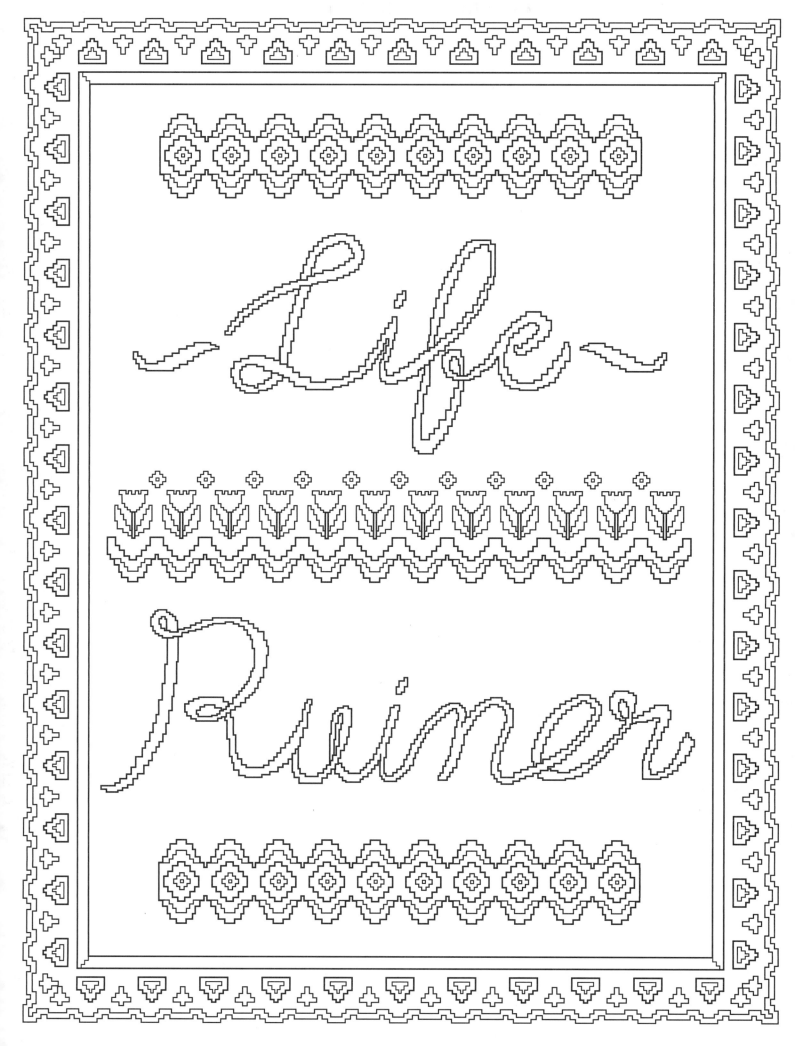

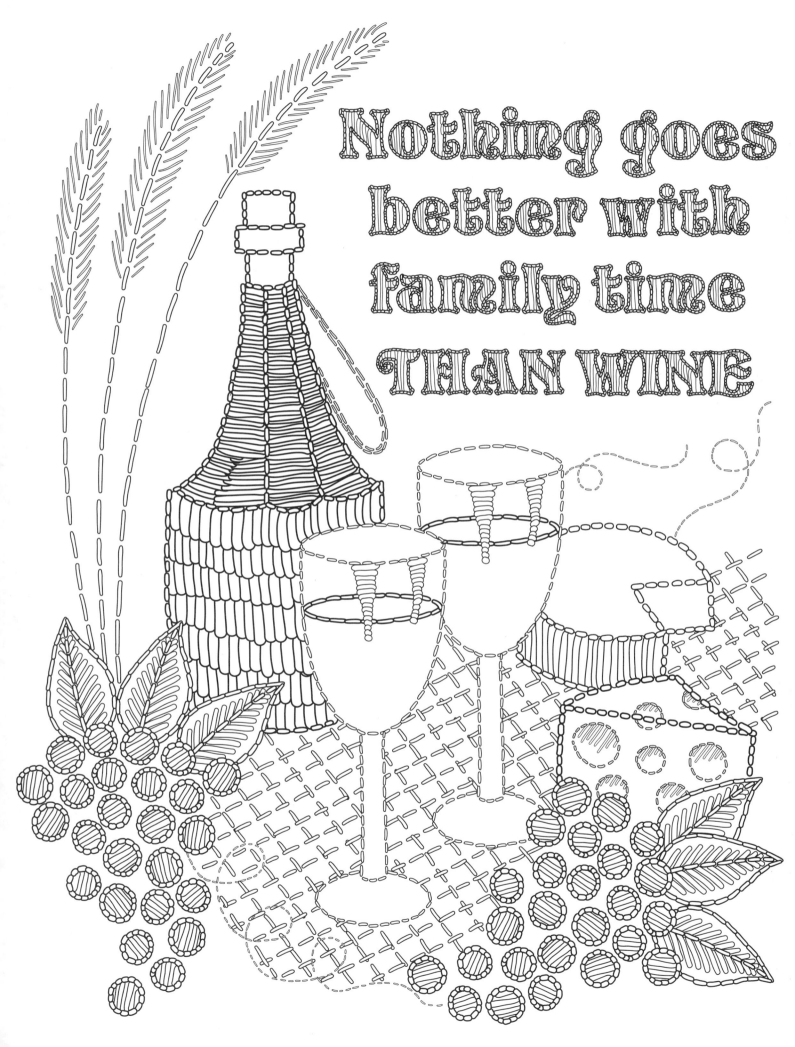

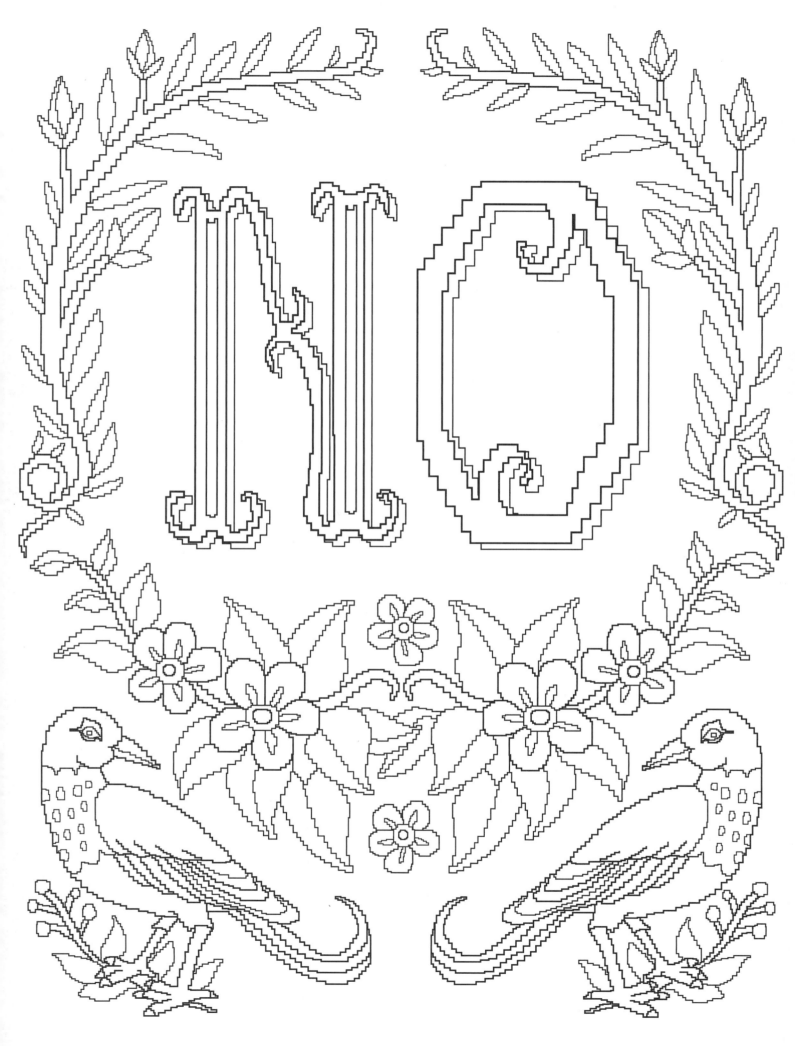

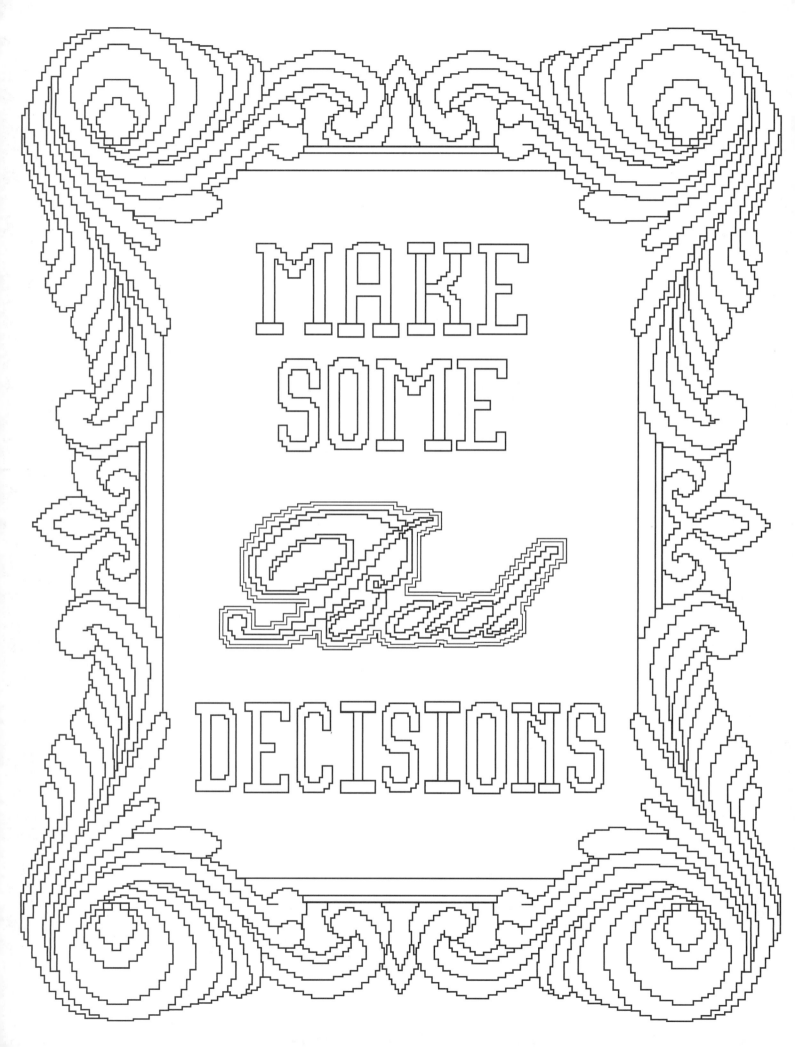

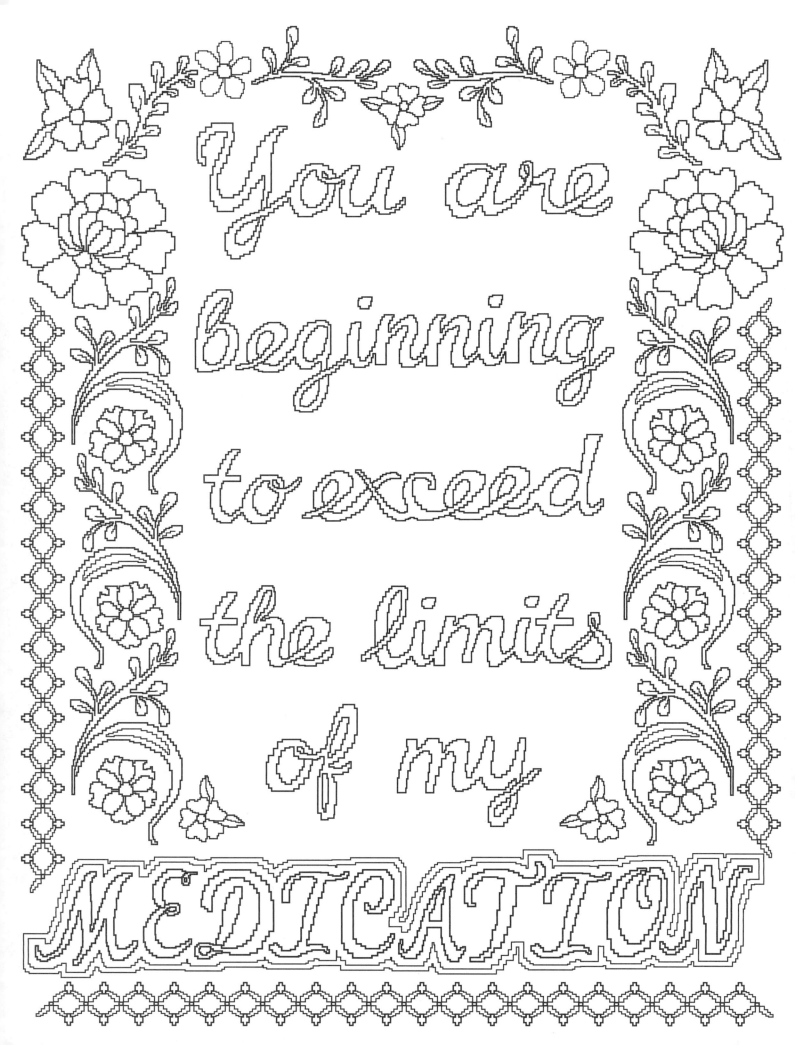

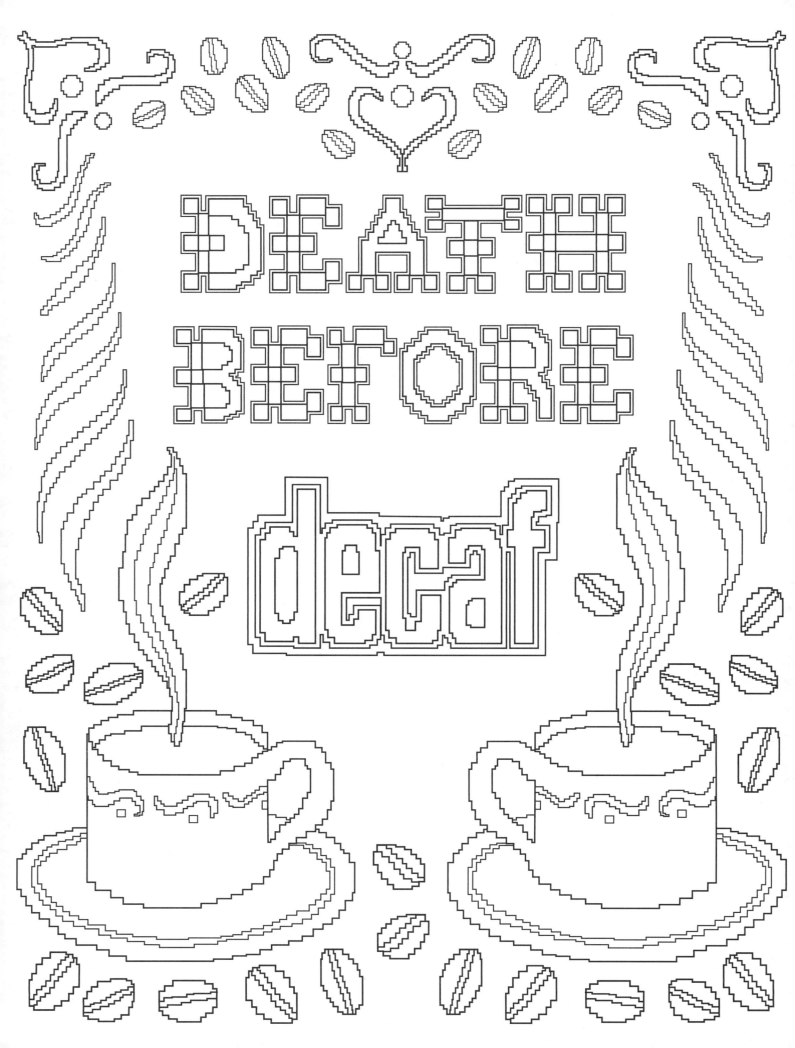

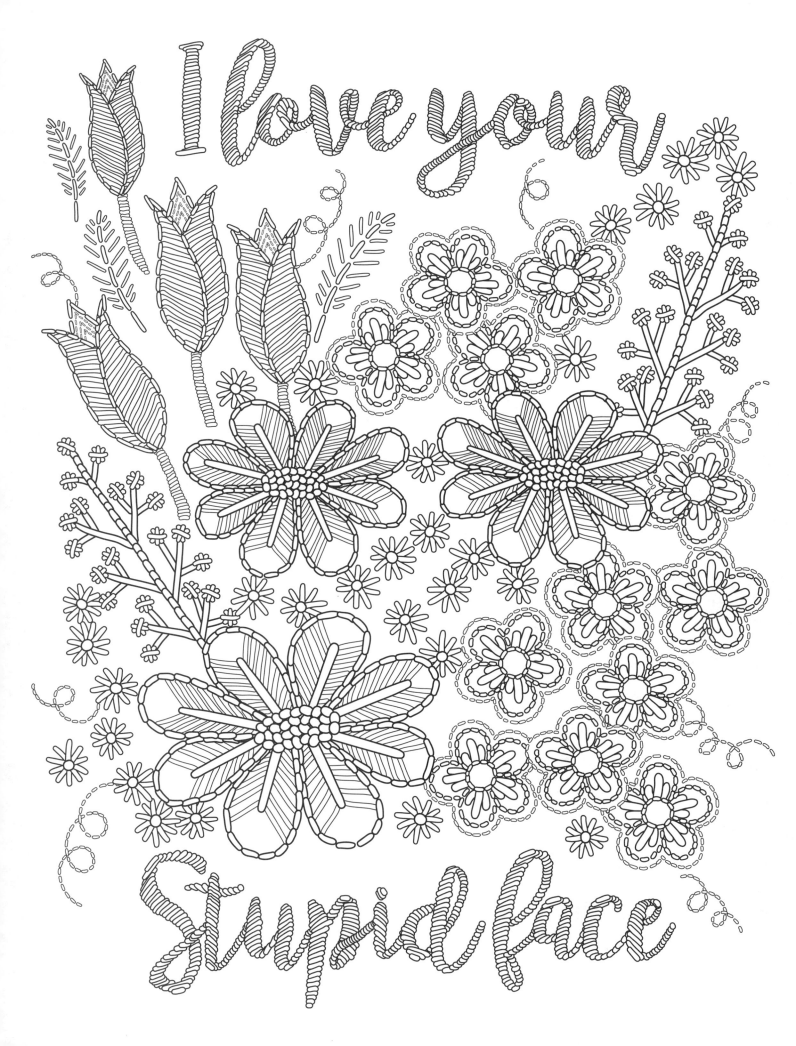

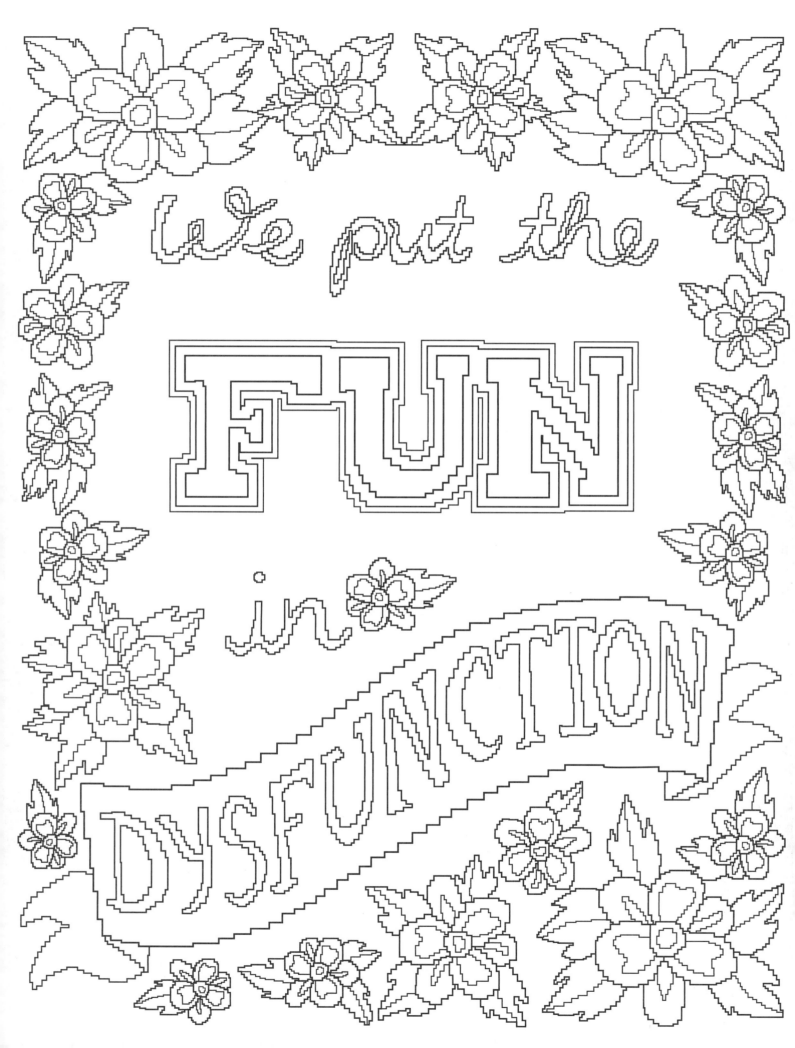

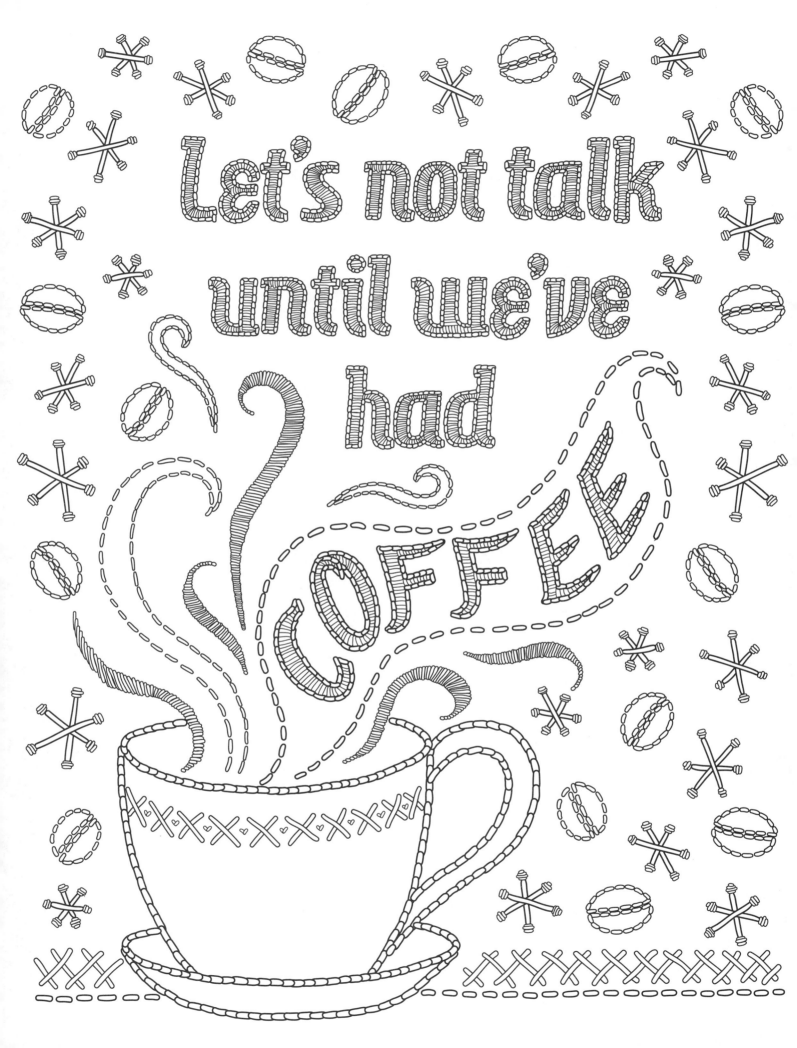

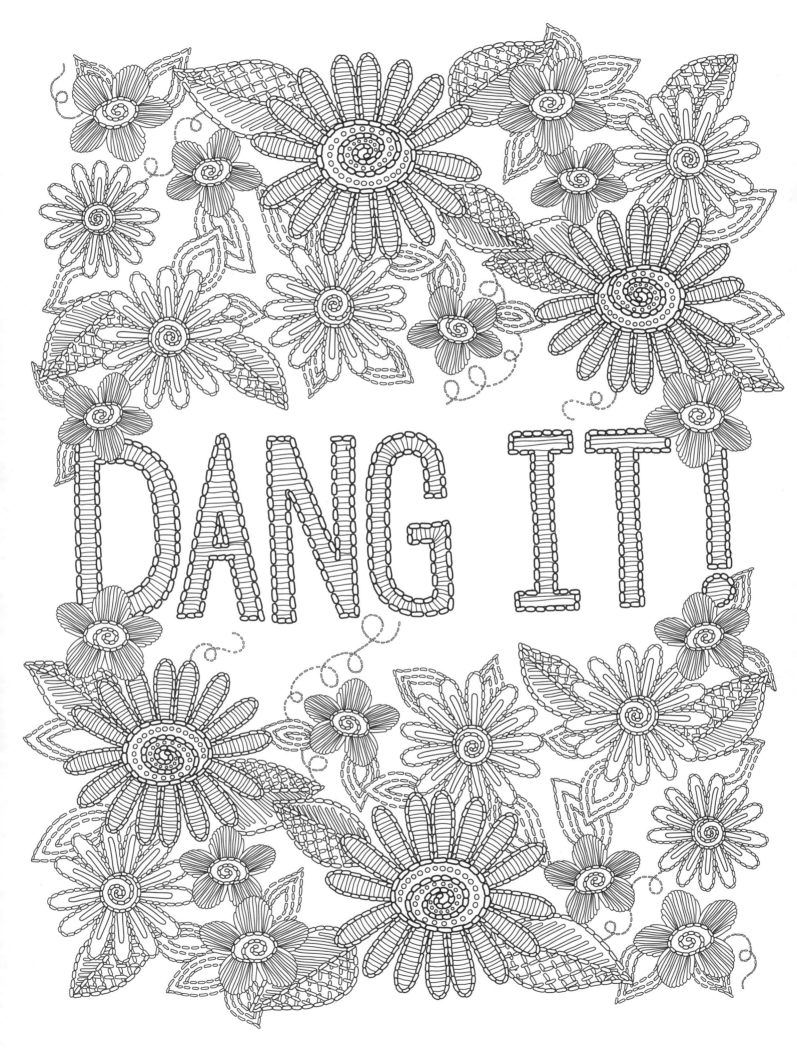

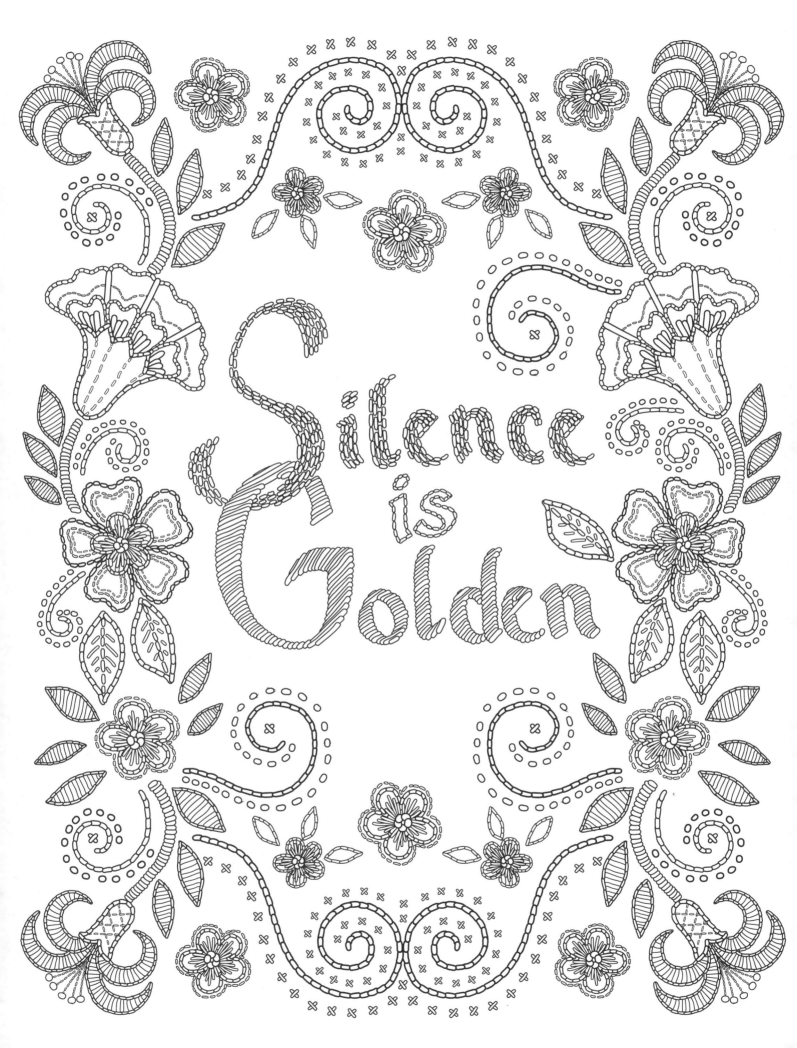

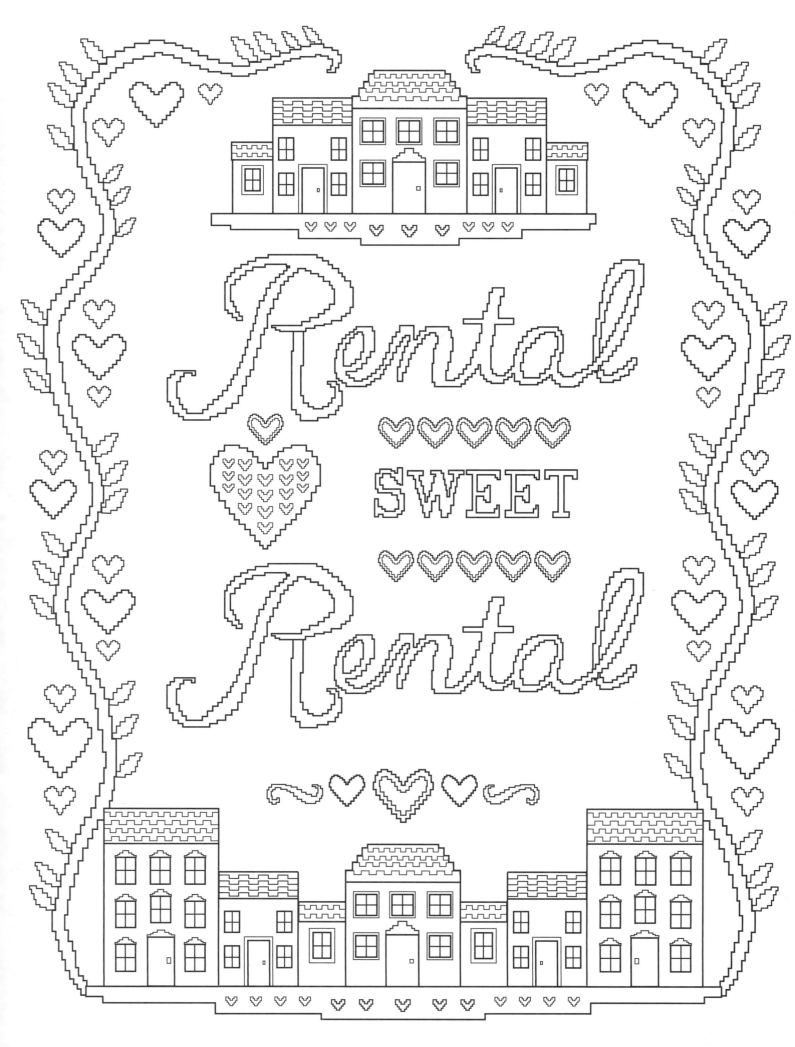

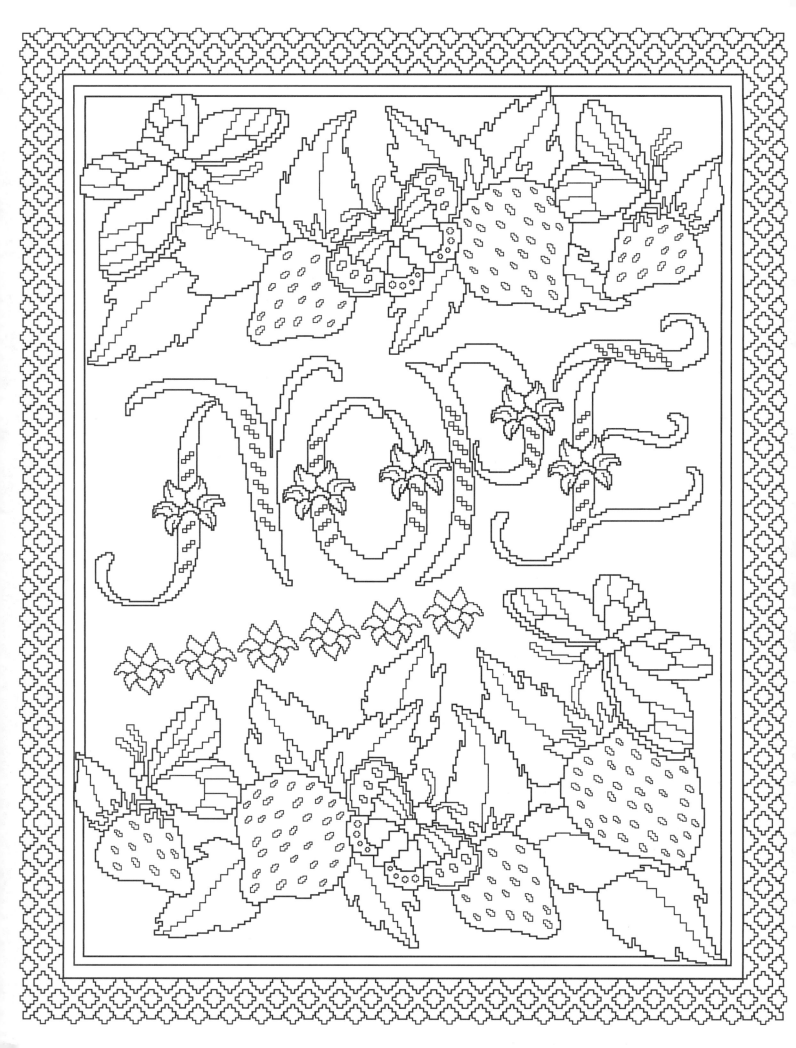

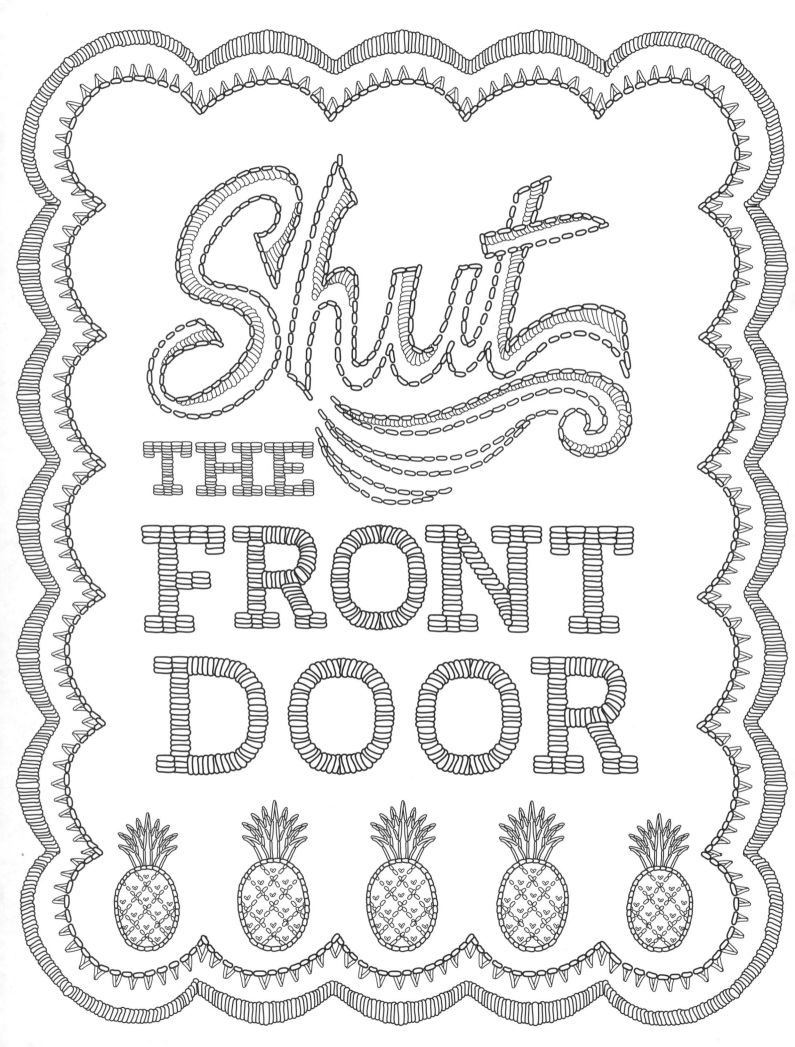

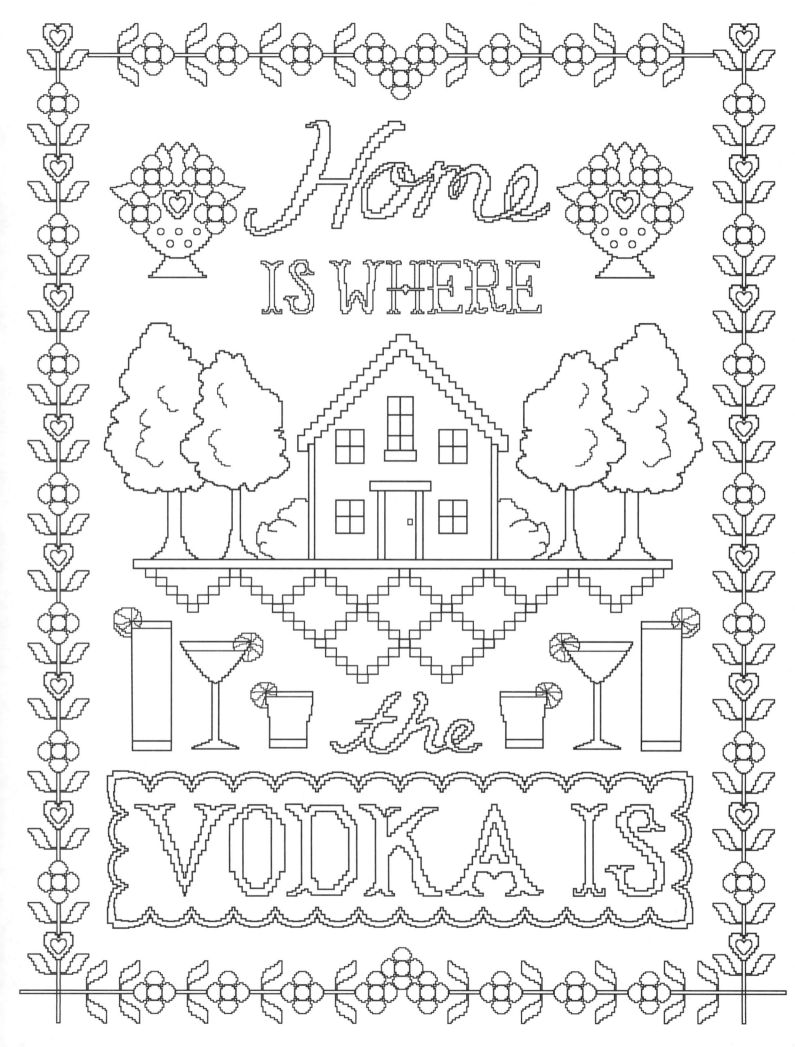

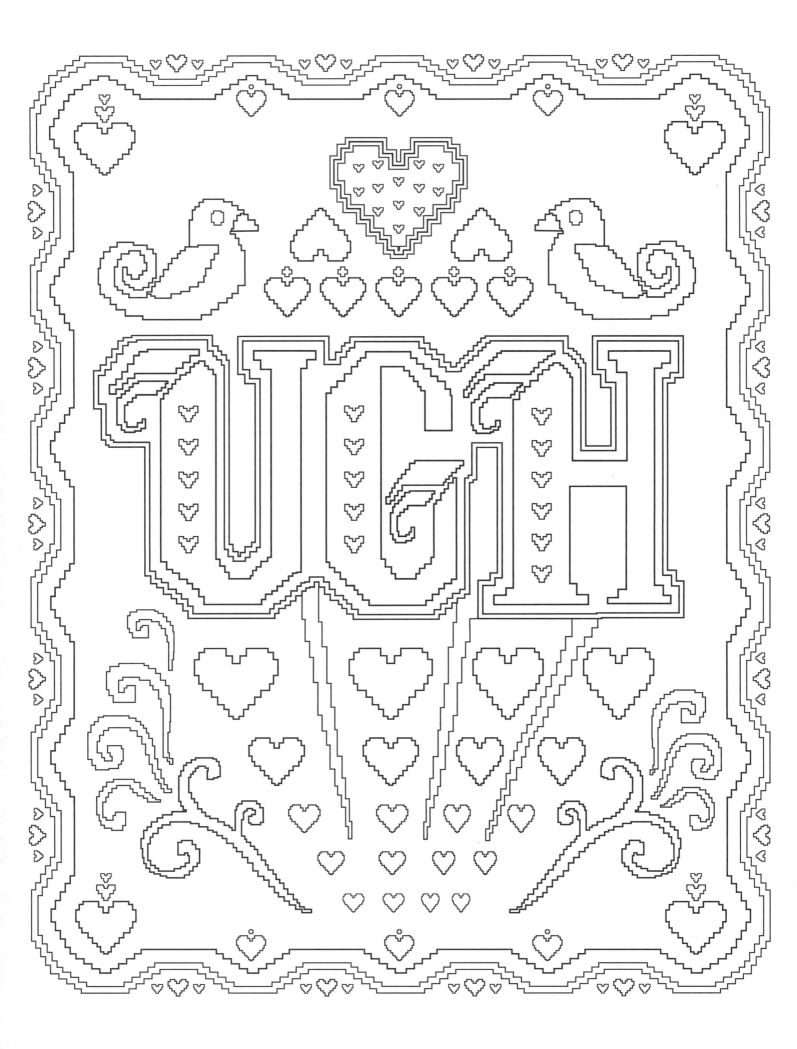

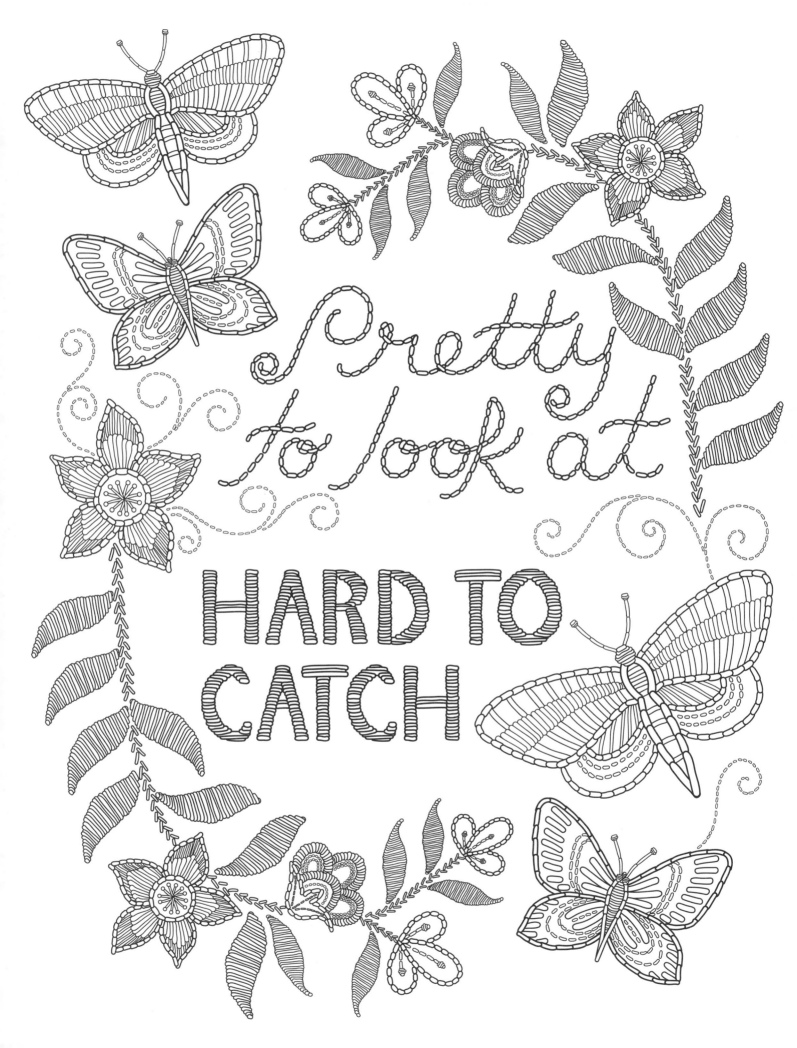

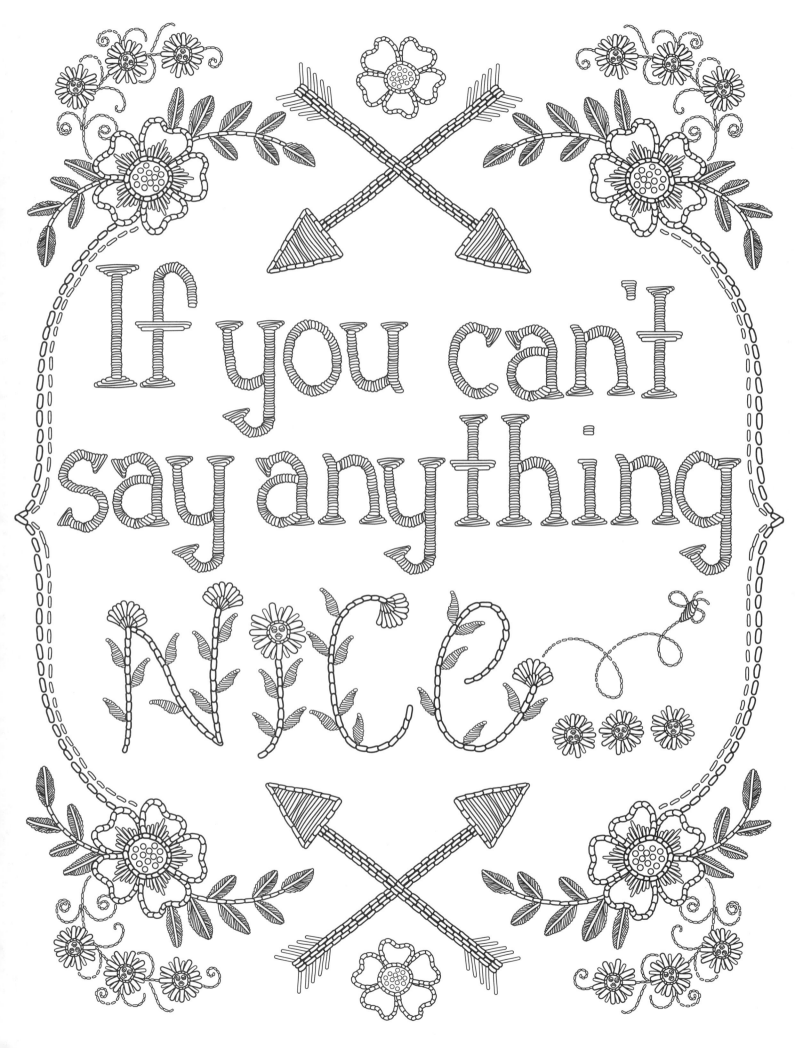

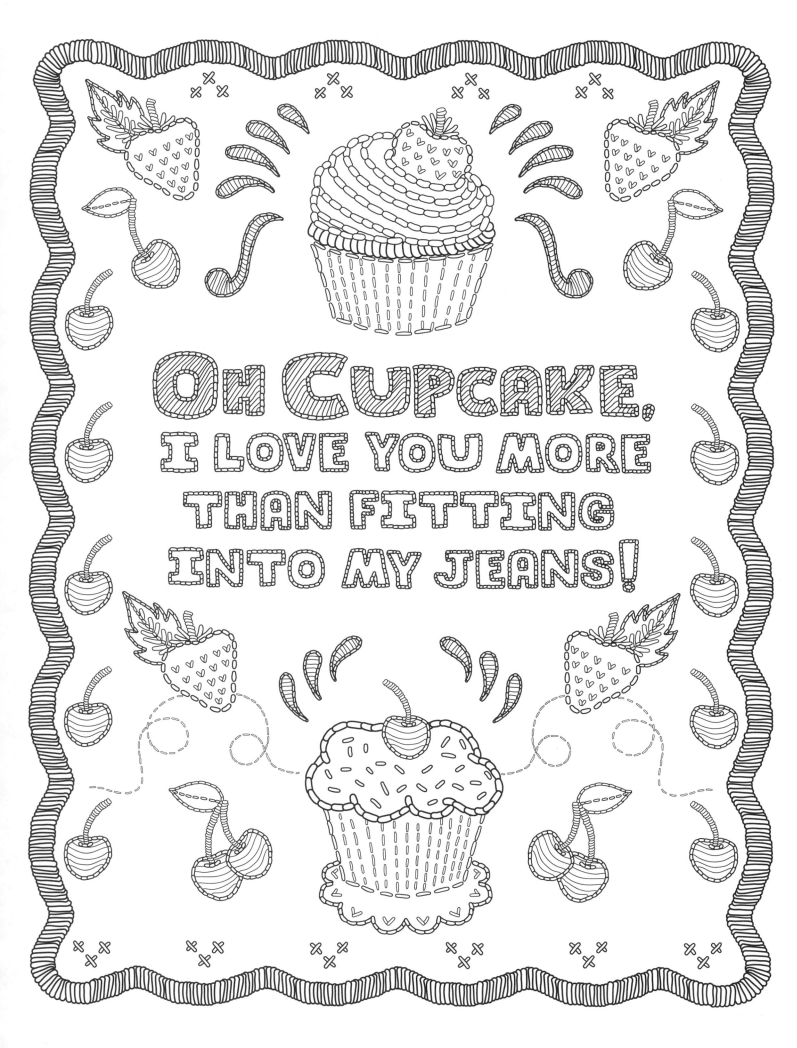

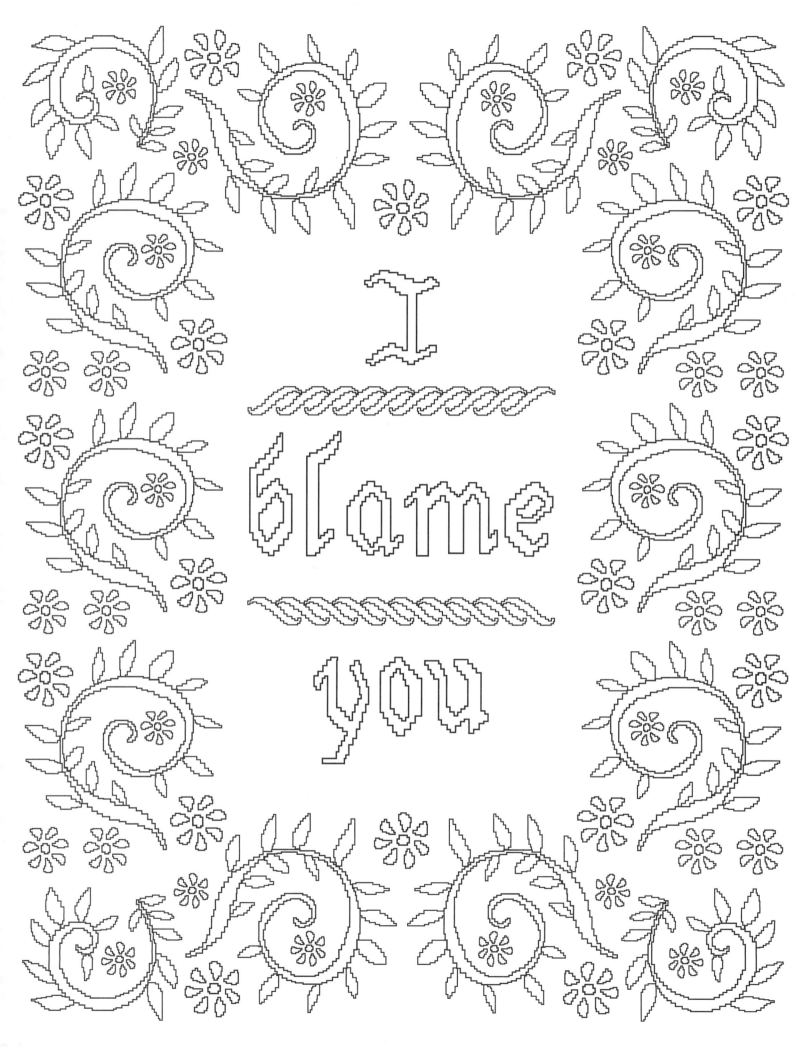

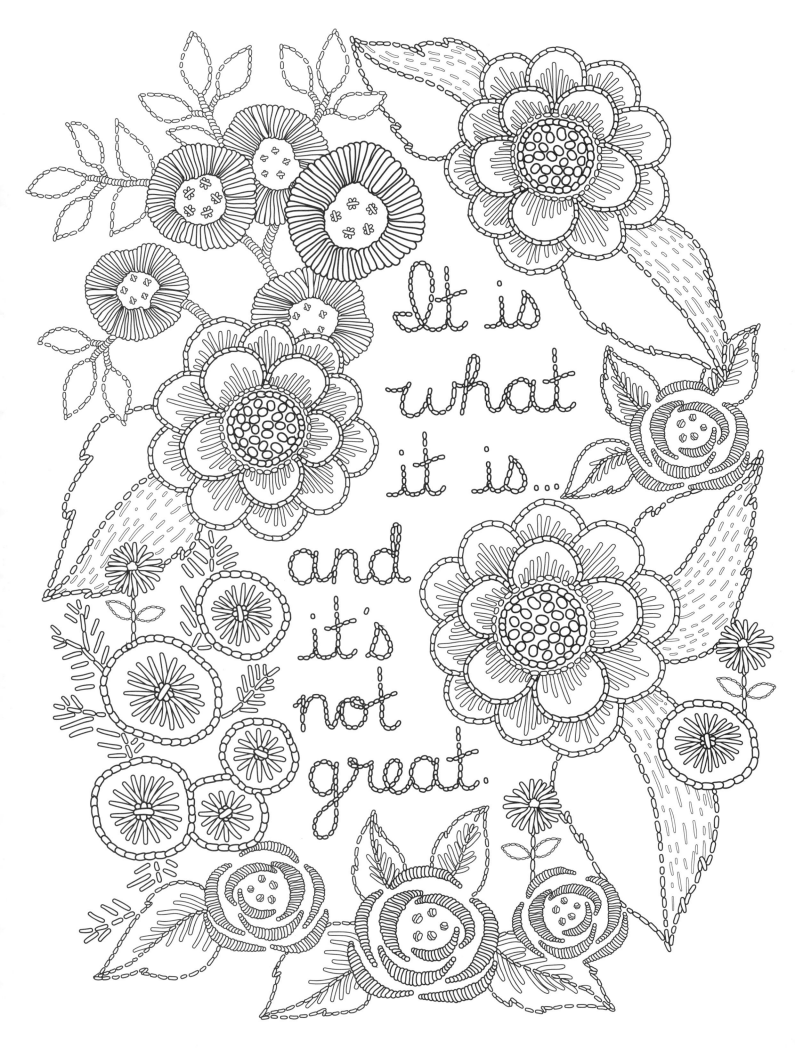

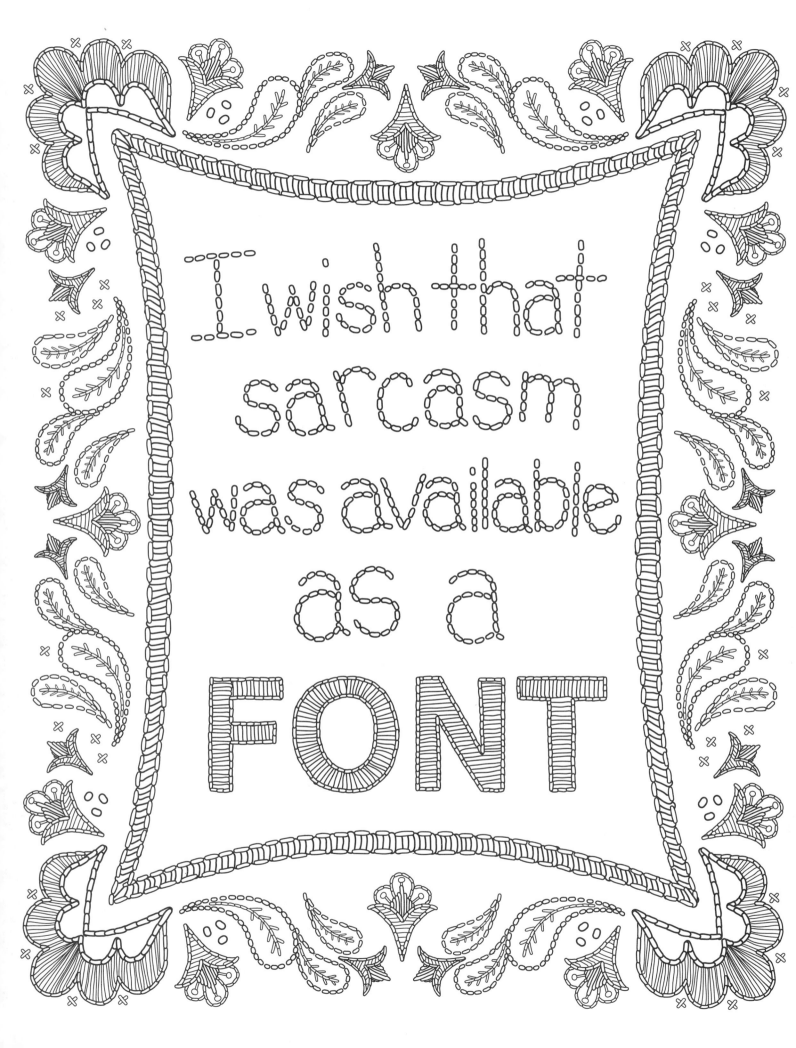

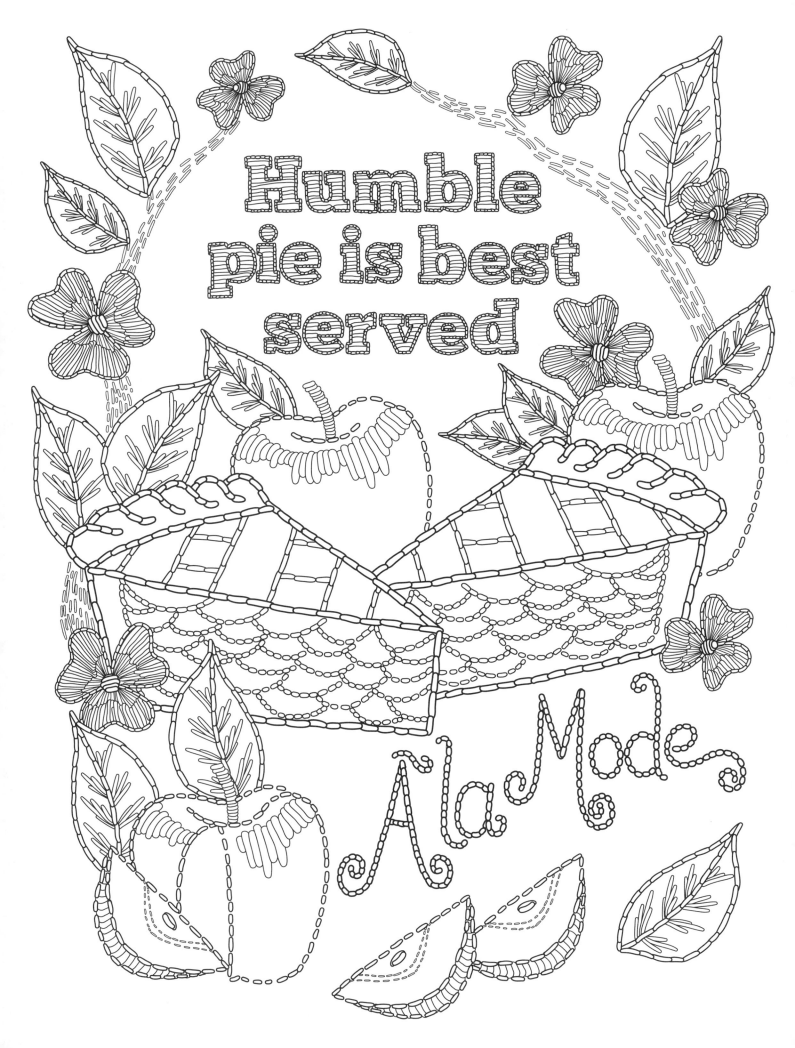

Humble pie is best served

A la Mode

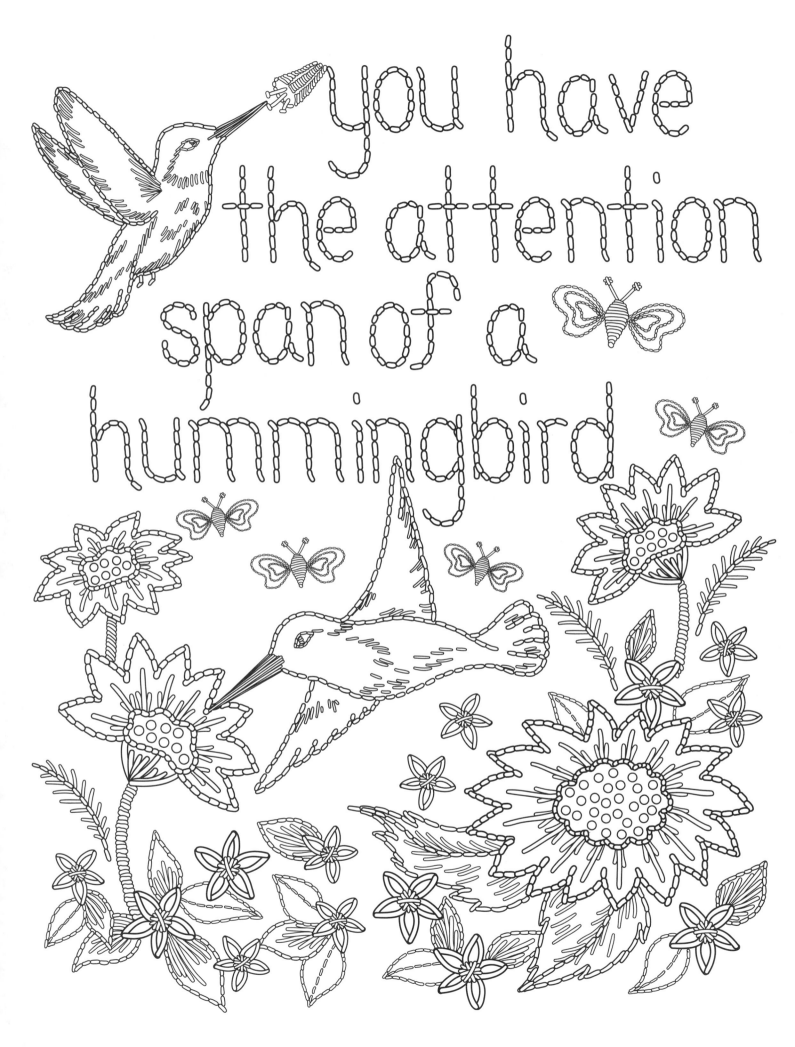

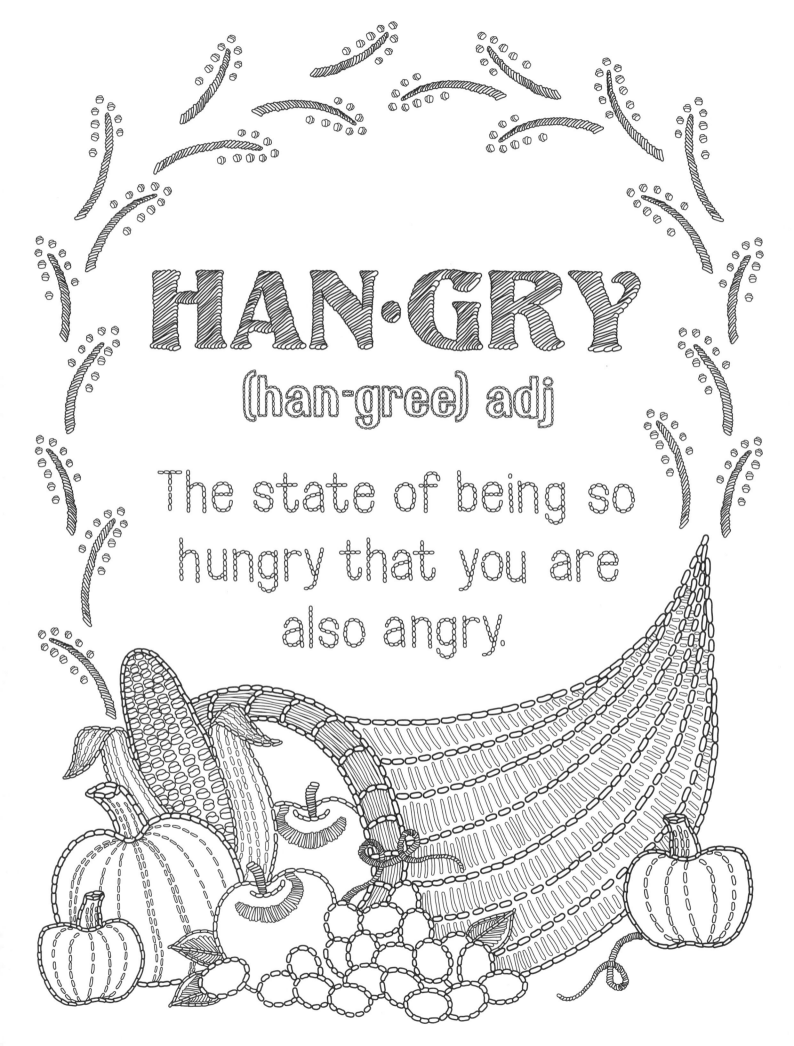

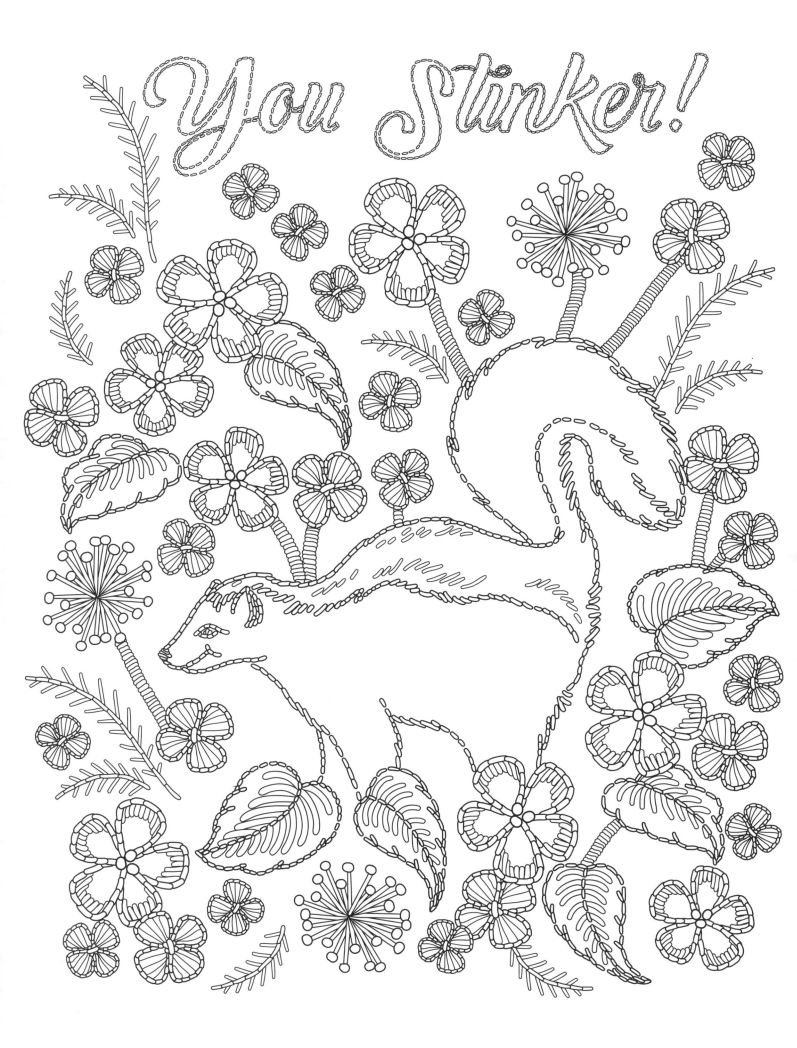

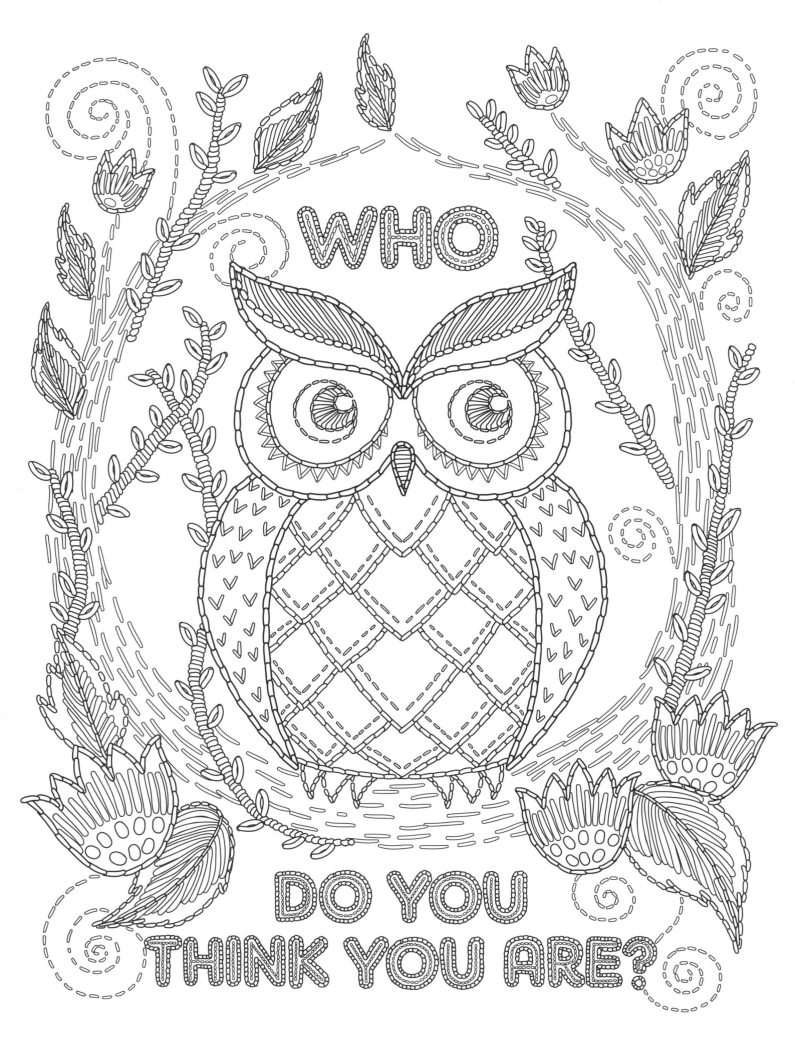

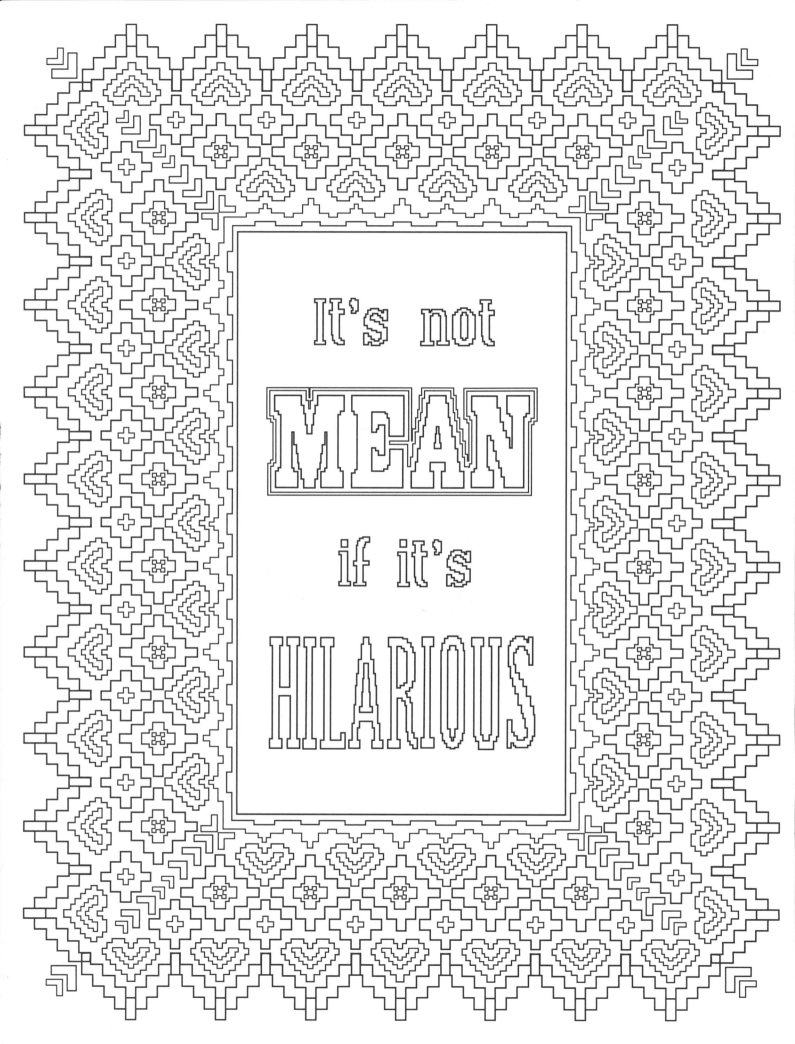

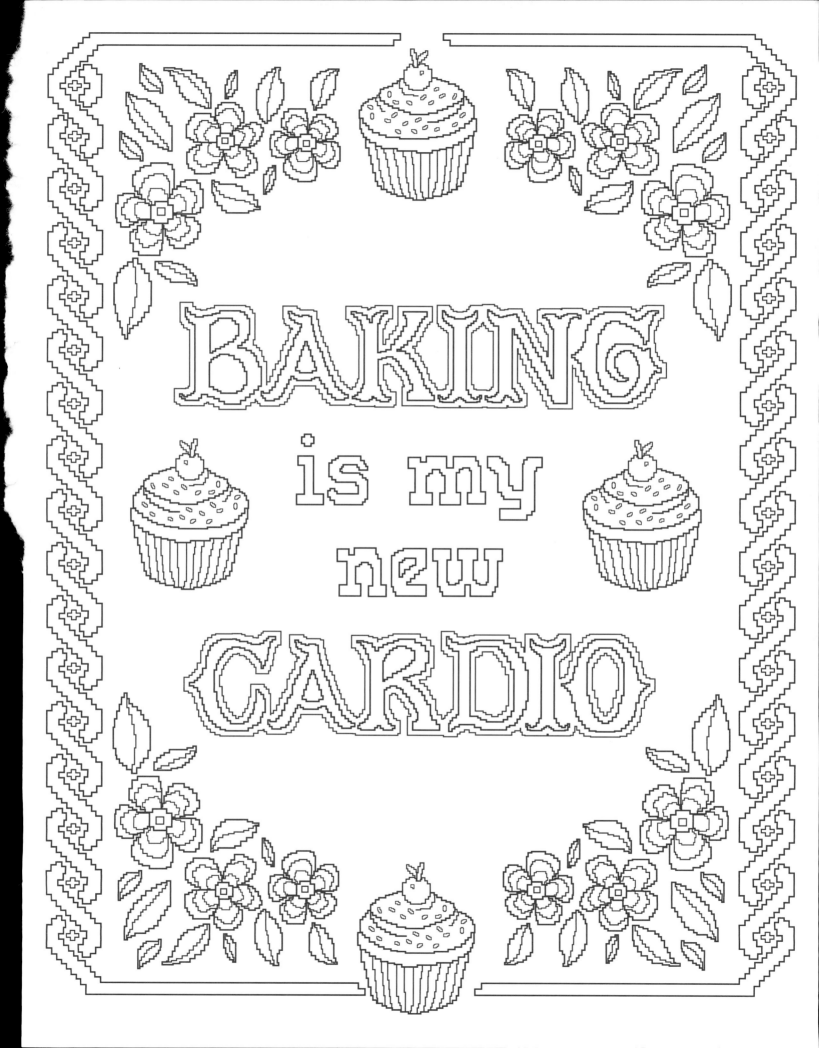

BAKING is my new CARDIO

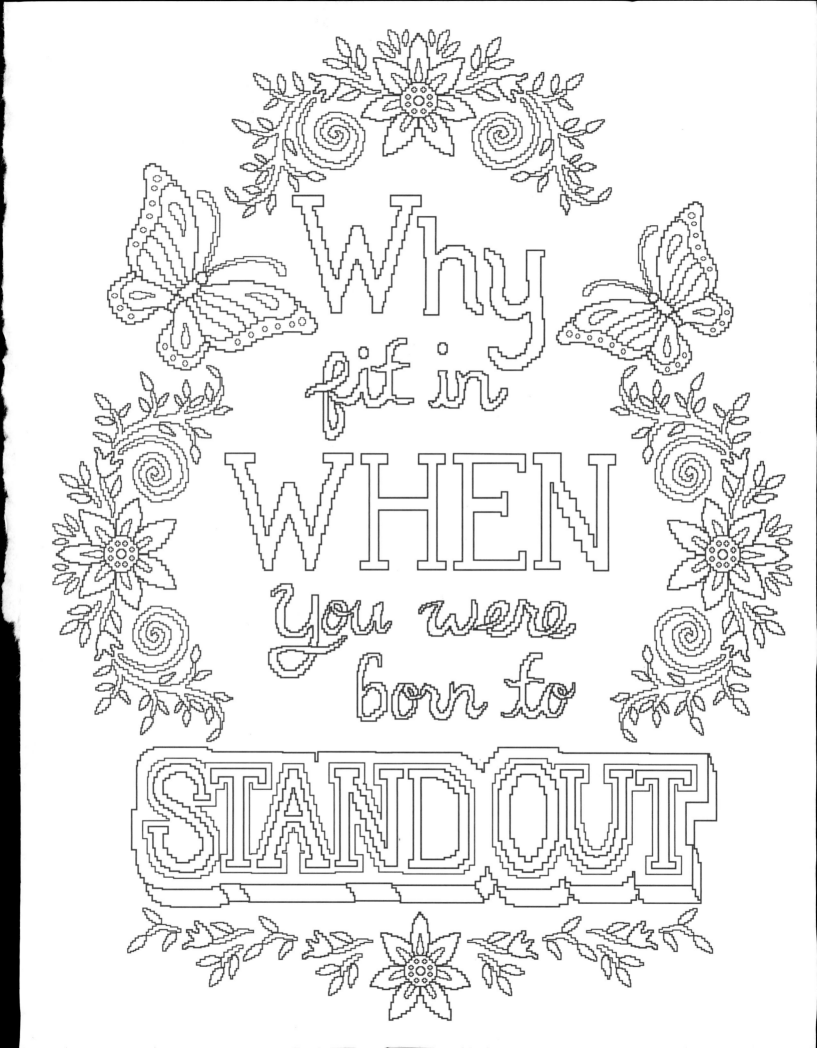